Salted
Plums

Salted Plums

a memoir of culture and identity

Alison Hồng Nguyễn Lihalakha

KAHANA PRESS

Published by Kahana Press, Honolulu, HI
www.kahanapress.com

Edited and designed by Girl Friday Productions
www.girlfridayproductions.com

Cover design: Kathleen Lynch
Project management: Sara Spees Addicott
Editorial production: Tiffany Taing, Abi Pollokoff
Image credits: cover © iStock Photo/Tverdohlib
Logo design: Ninja Designers

ISBN (paperback): 979-8-9853226-0-6
ISBN (ebook): 979-8-9853226-1-3

Library of Congress Control Number: 2022902359

For my husband and sons, and my mother

Contents

Author's Note. 1

Fake It till You Make It 3
Hot Chicken on a Road Trip 6
My Father: Fisherman, Drunk, Wife Beater,
    and Duck Killer 12
My Mother: Urban Farmer and the Queen's Mother. 24
Schoolyard Scuffle 32
Grilled Cheese Fantasies 39
Friendships Are Like Butter, Rice with Butter 49
Such Incivility, Dishonesty, and Thievery!. 57
Underdogs 62
Can't Fight This Feeling 67
Weekend Pursuits. 77
Spring Break with a Debutante. 84
Office Hours 91
Examining Cultural Identity 97
*69 106
Are You Lost, Dears?. 113
You Are Vietnamese If. 127
Returning to My ~~Motherland~~ Mother's Land 138
Dog Meat Served Here! 147
Just Wear a Pantsuit 157
History Lessons with a Side of Salted Plums 167

Is He Black? 171
Relationship Status: It's Complicated 183
It's Hong, Like Hong Kong 188
Bank Loan for a Getaway Boat. 194

Acknowledgments 207
About the Author 209

Author's Note

This book is a memoir. It reflects the author's present recollections of experiences over time. Some names and characteristics have been changed, some events have been compressed, and some dialogue has been re-created.

Fake It till You Make It

"Are you ready, Hong?"

I turned to face James, the director, and nodded. My hair and makeup were done, and I was in board shorts and a tank top. I was starring in a local television ad for an insurance company. This commercial was one of a few that I landed when I started auditioning in Hawaii. I had worked with James and the crew on other commercials. They were a fun bunch, and acting on the side beat sitting in the office at my day job, managing service contracts.

"Do you surf?" James asked as I leaned over to pick up the board from the grass.

"I took a lesson in Waikiki once."

"So you don't surf." Not a question.

"Nope." In my defense, I had managed to catch a few waves.

"Do you know how to hold a surfboard?"

I hesitated a beat.

"Sure," I replied. *Shouldn't have hesitated.*

"You don't sound sure. Here, give it to me."

"I can hold a surfboard," I insisted, turning to show him. "See?"

He took it from me. "Watch and learn." He jogged twenty feet down the slope, turned, and came back up. "Just like that, all right? Let's see you do it."

I took the cumbersome board back from James and tucked it under my right arm. It was heavy, and it wasn't even one of those really big longboards I had seen at the beach.

"Got it?" he asked. I nodded as I shifted to avoid dropping it. He looked as skeptical of my abilities as I felt. "OK, do some practice runs first."

I needed to make this seem like second nature. I had a gym membership and worked out several times a week. I was twenty-eight years old, 110 pounds, and looked fit, but I was not a natural athlete, nor a surfer. The board and I were competing with each other, and the board was winning. I took a deep breath, relaxed my shoulders, and launched into my mental pep talk. *You can do this. You can do this. It's just a surfboard. You are a surfer girl. Rock this. Fake it till you make it.* Down and back up I went.

With my practice runs over, it was time to be a surfer girl for the camera. *Rock this.* Baywatch. Baywatch. I tucked the board under my right arm and did my best impression of a surfer running toward the ocean. Surfer-girl me had time to surf because the claim on my automobile accident was being seamlessly handled by my insurance agent. I had an abundance of free time to catch the waves instead of worrying about repairs.

"Action!" James called out.

There were a couple dozen of us on a grassy knoll overlooking the ocean at the Kaka'ako Waterfront Park. The sun shone down, and the breeze kept us comfortable. Over a few takes, I hefted the board up and down the slight slope.

I didn't need to get anywhere near the water, thankfully, but this little exercise was exactly how I had been operating for most of my life. "Fake it till you make it" was my mantra. I said it to myself daily. Prominent Asians of my childhood were few and far between. I knew about Bruce Lee from my dad's movie collection and saw Connie Chung on the evening news. My everyday existence was filled mostly with people who looked nothing like me—in the grocery stores, shopping malls, and classrooms. These people were government and community leaders. They owned businesses, drove expensive cars, and lived in beautiful homes. They were Americans. They looked nothing like my family and me, so I didn't think being myself was an option.

When I was fourteen years old, the television series *21 Jump Street* came around. I was so excited to see Dustin Nguyễn, in his role as Harry Truman Ioki, that I searched for information about him in every teen magazine I could get my hands on. Coincidentally, both our families came through Fort Chaffee when we arrived in the United States. "We're related!" I would tell my friends, thinking that having a television star as a relative would make me cool. *Same last name. How could we not be related?*

Clearly, I had conflicting ideas about my identity. I simultaneously wanted to be white while trying to gain popularity by boasting about a television star who had the same last name I did. I was guarded and spent a lot of time curating my public persona, fearful that the real me was not good enough. If I didn't fit in, I would do everything I could, from changing my clothes to cutting my hair in a certain style, to make it seem like I belonged. If I didn't know how to do something, I would imitate others until I got it right.

I wasn't a surfer girl, but I could pretend to be one on television. I could fake it until I made it—or so I thought.

Hot Chicken on a Road Trip

I am originally from Việt Nam, but I have no memory of my motherland. I can't trace my own lineage back further than my great-grandparents, and I couldn't tell you their names if you were to ask. Faced with life under Communist rule, my parents fled our home country in 1975, at the end of the Vietnam War, known to those in Việt Nam as the American War (or more formally, the Resistance War against America). My siblings and I were swept up in our parents' arms and ushered onto a rickety wooden boat to a new life in a foreign land. We were taken to Guam and ended up in Fort Chaffee, Arkansas, for a few months before we moved to Lawton, Oklahoma. We eventually settled in Panama City, Florida, a sleepy little town about a thirty-minute drive from white-sand beaches. In a community of a few hundred Catholic Vietnamese families, we held on to not just our faith but also our heritage through the events and activities we took part in at our little church. I didn't see Việt Nam again until I was twenty-six years old, and that meant there were a lot of years in between when I struggled to figure out who I was and where I belonged.

I spoke Vietnamese at home with my family. We ate rice at every meal. On Sundays, we ate *phở*, the traditional noodle soup in a rich beef broth that takes hours to perfect. My mom started cooking the bones on Saturday nights. On Tết, to usher in the new year, we dressed in our finest outfits and visited relatives, eager to receive the little red envelopes that held crisp dollar bills and two-dollar coins from our elders. And every autumn, we would celebrate the rice harvest—even though harvesting was something none of us actually did—by lighting lanterns and eating mooncakes.

One year for Tết Trung Thu, the Mid-Autumn Festival, many of us kids from the Vietnamese church community saved up empty soda cans to make lanterns. My older brother, Cường; older sister, Hà; and I, along with other children from church, used knives to cut slits around the sides from top to bottom. (My three younger brothers and younger sister were too little for such a dangerous task.) We squashed the cans just enough so that the slits bowed outward in the midsection. Inside went a little votive candle or a cut piece of a taper. We hung our soda-can lanterns from twigs and rods using string or yarn, whatever we could find.

Father An had taught us folk songs as part of our church youth-group activities. With our lanterns in hand, we marched from the churchyard to the housing project where most of the Vietnamese families lived. We must have been quite a sight, about five dozen of us kids, with our cantankerous singing and our swaying lanterns, marching through the neighborhood in the evening, taking up the roads and sidewalks with our boisterous celebration of the autumn moon when we should have been eating dinner.

I remember feeling joy in the songs and laughing as the lights in our lanterns flickered in the streets and evening took us from twilight to dusk, swallowing us up while amplifying our noisy happiness. This was a celebration before I realized that what we were doing was different or odd; it was a celebration I took part in without shame, without feeling any self-consciousness.

* * *

The earliest memory I have is of sucking on a fish when I was around five or six years old. My dad, like his brothers and cousins, was a fisherman. Along the coast of the Gulf of Mexico in the Florida Panhandle where we lived, my dad trawled the open waters for fish and shrimp while my mom took care of us kids.

My mother and father came from humble backgrounds. They married when they were fifteen and nineteen, respectively. I don't think they were educated beyond elementary school in their small villages in Việt Nam, but even as a child, I could feel the desperation in their old-country ways, and I knew I wanted more out of life. They always worked hard and looked tired. They never smiled and seemed resigned to a life of struggle.

Despite our relative poverty, I remember eating seafood all the time and getting candy when my father would return from his nights out at sea. The pace of life was slow, and the future seemed so far off. We went to school, church, and the beach. On American Independence Day, we would sit at the dock where my dad's boat was tethered and watch the fireworks rain down over the water. Times were hard, but we had somehow joined the multitudes of Vietnamese refugees who had transitioned and adjusted to living in America.

In Panama City, we lived in a government housing project that consisted of duplexes along a road that ran in the shape of a horseshoe. Streets were neat and clean, yards burst with blue hydrangeas and pink azaleas in the summertime, and sidewalks were shaded by the wide-reaching arms of tall oak trees heavy with acorns. Backyards consisted of lush vegetable and herb gardens. My mom and her friends grew rows and rows of eggplant, cucumbers, bitter melons, Thai chilies, basil, and tomatoes. It was subsidized housing for the poor, a mix of white people, Black people, and newly arrived Vietnamese refugees, but pride of ownership was still important to the families living there. With only one uncle and his family residing in the same city, we were separated from the rest of my dad's abundantly numbered side of the family by a couple of state lines. We took road trips from Florida to our grandparents' place in Biloxi, Mississippi, so we could visit them and our countless aunts, uncles, and cousins. Our family of nine would pile into the car, a black Ford LTD sedan affectionately called the Limo, and given the lack of road rules about child safety in the early 1980s, every nook and cranny of the vehicle was filled for our interstate journey. The younger ones were lucky if they scored a seat instead of being relegated to the floorboards. The Limo had one long, bench-like front seat, so there was no popping your head in between the driver and passenger to see what was going on up ahead. I would lie across the back dash, pressed against the rear window, watching other cars come up behind us as we cruised along the highway.

On one of these trips, we stopped at Popeyes for lunch. It was a rare trip where my mom hadn't packed an assortment of Vietnamese foods—*thịt kho* (braised pork) with rice or *bánh mì* (baguette sandwiches). After a quick debate over who could best represent our culinary interests, I was dispatched with Dad to go in and order lunch. By around age seven, I was on my way to becoming the go-to interpreter and translator for my parents. Dad and I stepped into the wondrous establishment that was Popeyes Famous Fried Chicken. Every table, bench, and window gleamed in the midday sun, and I had nothing but wide eyes. Being so poor and with a family so big, the world of fast food was a luxury foreign to us.

With Dad at my side, I tentatively approached the counter to place our order. The lady acknowledged the items and then asked, "Do you want it hot?"

I looked at her blankly, baffled. *Did people eat fried chicken cold?*

Not getting an immediate answer, she sighed and repeated, "Do you want it hot or not?"

I turned to my dad to relay in Vietnamese what she was asking us. We looked at each other, and he nudged me to respond in the affirmative.

"Um . . . yes?" I replied. And then, with more conviction, "Yes, yes, we want it hot."

While Dad paid, I glanced past the cashier to the kitchen beyond, trying to spot refrigerators full of cold chicken, ready for the asking. When our order was presented, Dad and I returned to the Limo with our bounty.

Untangling limbs to claim lunch, my brothers and sisters and I did what any large and unruly family does—we grabbed whatever share of the meal we could get our hands on and started eating. The chorus of negative reviews came all at once from the little ones.

"It's spicy!"

"I don't like it spicy!"

"My mouth is on fire!"

"Water!"

It was a cacophony of complaints in Vietnamese. We could eat any spicy Việt dish, but now we couldn't handle spicy American fried chicken.

I looked at my dad in confusion, and then it hit me. I blurted, "She should've asked if we wanted it spicy!" My siblings and parents had no idea what I was going on about, so I explained that the lady inside had asked if we wanted our chicken hot. In Vietnamese, *hot* and *spicy* are assigned distinct terms, leaving no doubt as to which is which. You say *cay* when you mean spicy, and you say *nóng* when you mean hot. Exasperated and deflated, I concluded with, "Only she meant spicy, not hot."

The English language can be so complicated. Lunch had

been foiled by a three-letter word with more than one meaning. Dad and I went back in to order another batch of fried chicken. I felt the flush of embarrassment on my cheeks as I approached the lady again. "We don't want it *spicy*," I added curtly at the end of our new order, not giving her the chance to dupe me again.

We ate lots of fried chicken that day, and despite all the complaints about the first order being too spicy, I don't recall there being any leftovers.

My Father: Fisherman, Drunk, Wife Beater, and Duck Killer

My dad died suddenly two months before I turned nine. He was thirty-seven. He had been working for months to finish building his fishing boat. Had just completed it, maybe even that afternoon. Hadn't even taken it out into the Gulf of Mexico.

It was late at night, after ten o'clock, when his heart stopped. My siblings and I woke up, roused out of bed by the commotion. Someone called 911. I don't know who.

The siren disrupted our street's nighttime calm as the ambulance pulled up in front of our house. The emergency responders rushed through the front door and into the bedroom in the back. I looked out the large windows of our living room, gazing into the darkness, which was cut by the white of the ambulance and the red bulbs on top as they turned around and around, flashing in their silent urgency. Our neighbors pulled back their curtains to see what was happening. I imagine they only felt sorry for us, because a middle-of-the-night ambulance never bodes well.

I don't know where Mom was exactly, probably in the hallway outside the master bedroom. All of us kids were in the living room, a few of us standing, some of us sitting on the orange and brown sofa. We were like the patchwork on a worn-out quilt on the verge of unraveling. We waited silently for the paramedics to come out from the back bedroom where Dad slept, each of us taking turns being cast in red from the lights of the ambulance outside. My four brothers (Cường, age ten; Mark, five; Tiến, four; and Doan, just three) didn't know what was happening. My sisters (Hà, age thirteen, and Hạnh, seven) and I didn't know what was happening. We didn't realize our lives were changing forever in those moments.

The paramedics wheeled Dad out on the gurney and took him away in the ambulance. I didn't know he was dead then, that the next morning he would not be waking up to tend to his fishing boat, and that in fact this was his last time leaving our house. The doctor at the hospital declared him dead a minute after midnight, so even now, I'm not sure exactly which day to say he died on.

The funeral was a massive affair. My dad's side of the family swarmed down to Panama City from their homes in Biloxi and Mobile. Fortunate and financially stable Americans get together for reunions to celebrate familial bonds and enjoy a nice big barbecue lunch. We were Vietnamese and poor, so our reunions were mostly at funerals, with the occasional wedding here and there. I think every cousin I had living in the United States came to bury my dad.

Vietnamese funerals are noisy and peculiar affairs. Immediate and extended family members line up alongside the casket, taking up every bit of space around it. Women weep and wail and plead at the top of their lungs with the deceased. "Oh, why did you have to leave us?" "What are we to do without you?" "I cannot go on alone!" "Please, please come back!" These lamentations are heartbreaking, even for those who don't understand what is being said. The one-sided conversation goes on and on, interrupted only by prayers or when someone suffers

dehydration or exhaustion and passes out. Widows throw themselves on their dead husbands' coffins, in a desperate attempt
either to join them in the afterlife or to bring them back. My aunt
did just that when her husband, my dad's younger brother Chú
Hiền, died the year before. Then she promptly fainted, and her
brothers-in-law swooped in to catch her.

Everyone wears black, except the deceased's immediate
family—they wear white muslin tunics and pajama-style pants
over other clothes. I learned that the Vietnamese also used to
wear white pointed hats, similar to what the American KKK
members wear, except without the face covering with eyeholes
cut out. However, white, for Vietnamese people, symbolizes
death, not joy. (I don't think it took us Vietnamese Americans
long to shed our pointed hats, what with the connotations they
hold in American history. And we embraced white wedding
gowns with fervor—the puffier the skirt, the better.)

Photos and videos are taken of every detail and every moment. The images and scenes are keepsakes, alongside baby pictures and locks of hair. The photos would be shared all around
with family and friends. We would eventually sit and watch the
video, commenting on the events and the attendees as if we were
watching sports.

At these funerals, we children stand stone-faced, with our
white fabric bands wrapped around our heads in our show of
mourning. Everyone is very sad, yet the air is charged, as if
we are at a big farewell party for the deceased. Even though
we're Roman Catholics, the weeping and pleading feel very un-
Catholic to me, but maybe that's why those jags are interrupted
by prayers.

It was 1982 when my father passed away. Still early in the
years of Vietnamese people living in America. I was only eight,
but as I observed the women wailing and fainting, I imagined
the American funeral home workers were filling up their memory banks with tales of the strange Vietnamese funerals they

witnessed. If they'd had smartphones back then, I'm certain the spectacle of our grief, so foreign to them, would have ended up online one way or another. Slightly mortified, I felt it would have been unfair for outsiders, as I viewed these funeral home workers, to judge us for our display of sadness. Grief manifests itself in many ways, and this was ours.

I came across the video of my dad's funeral years later, when I was in high school. Mom had kept it in a box she'd moved with us from Florida to Kansas. Mom had taken a trip to the Vatican to see Pope John Paul II and kiss his ring. I took the opportunity to rummage through her bedroom closet to see what I could find. There were some other family videos in the box, along with the one documenting Dad's funeral. Our family's history, stored in tattered cardboard, recorded on tapes that would eventually become obsolete, lost to history. The thought of watching Dad's funeral brought me no comfort, so I tossed it back in where I found it. I had been there, trailing in the back of the procession out of the church. I remembered it. All the wailing and somberness. I didn't need to relive it.

*   *   *

One of the fondest memories I have of my father is of him bringing York Peppermint Patties home for us after his fishing trips. The little shop at the dock sold these individually wrapped treats. Cool, fresh mint cream encased in a delicate outer layer of thin dark chocolate. I loved the little patties as a kid, and even now, when I eat one, I close my eyes and think of dear old Dad. When the mint hits my tongue, I take in a long, deep breath, and it feels like I'm clearing away all the bad stuff, including his death and everything bad that came after it, because he's there in that minty inhale and exhale. He's part of me still, and the fresh feeling is him taking away all the sadness, leaving me clean and whole again.

In my mind's eye, I see tangles of fishing nets all over the floor of the dock. Knotty webs of loops that would stretch for what seemed like miles when I pulled on them. Bright green when new, then browned and turning gray from exposure to the sea and sun over time. Seaweed and the occasional shell clung in clumps here and there. I can see my dad sitting in the middle of it all, mending the tears, preparing for his next trip out into the Gulf. In my youth, I marveled that my dad could sew, never mind that it wasn't actually sewing.

Despite growing up in Florida, none of us kids had taken swimming lessons, which, in retrospect, was a horrible thing, considering we spent a lot of time on the dock and the beach. It was a wonder we didn't drown, but Dad was an excellent swimmer. I was so proud of him for knowing how to swim. I always felt like he was a superstar when I witnessed him in command of the water, diving confidently off the side of the boat and gliding through the Gulf. I loved watching as he deftly checked for damage and cleaned barnacles off the hull.

My father was one of many Vietnamese fishermen who worked in the Gulf of Mexico after fleeing Việt Nam. One of his brothers took up residence in Panama City, and we grew up alongside his four children, our closest cousins on my dad's side of the family. The rest of my dad's brothers and sisters settled in Biloxi, Mississippi. Along the shores of the Gulf, more Vietnamese families established themselves from the mid-1970s on, eventually becoming a large presence among those who trawled for shrimp and caught fish, feeding into the seafood industry in the Southeast.

National Geographic ran a piece about my dad's side of the family in September 1981, titled "The Wanderers from Vung Tau: Troubled Odyssey of Vietnamese Fishermen." Senior staff writer Harvey Arden and photographer Steve Wall had gone down to Biloxi and interviewed the Vietnamese fishermen at a time when tensions were building between locals and newly arrived refugees jockeying for their share of shrimp. The new-comers were fishing north to south while the locals went east to west, causing trawls and nets to tangle. Local fishing rules were not understood or followed until tempers flared and community leaders stepped in.

I was in my mid-forties when I discovered this relic. The hardworking people in the photos were people I knew in my youth. The faces were those of my paternal aunt, whom I called Bác Thái, working the shrimp processing line, and my paternal cousin's grandparents on her mother's side, sitting at their small kitchen table as they ate bowls of rice and soup. That article was evidence that my family, Vietnamese refugees who had arrived in the late 1970s, were truly part of the American fabric, though we were still new and viewed as outsiders.

I didn't know this while growing up, but my dad's side of the family, as large as it was and always growing, likely contrib-uted significantly to the growth of the Gulfport-Biloxi area from the late 1970s to 1990. My mom's brother, Cậu Tuyển, estimated that our extended family probably made up three-quarters of the Vietnamese population in Biloxi. The numbers grew as many of my paternal cousins got married and had kids of their own. They followed in their parents' footsteps, working on the boats, and when our parents and grandparents started thinning out due to illness and death, my cousins shifted from fishing to laboring on the receiving docks, shucking oysters and peeling shrimp. They eventually made their way into the casinos that opened in the 1990s, working as dealers, kitchen help, and housekeeping staff, but as time went on, the younger generation left to seek opportu-nities elsewhere, like North Carolina and Texas.

*   *   *

Our life in Florida was slower and quieter than that of our Mississippi counterparts. With just my dad's brother, whom we called Chú Quân, in Panama City, we stuck with his family for get-togethers during holidays and on Sundays, allowing us to grow up alongside our cousins Thu, Thủy, Minh, and Hương. Weekends were filled with church activities, then perhaps a trip to the beach when time permitted.

On a few occasions, Dad had taken us kids to Miracle Strip Amusement Park along the main beach road. My older sister, Hà, and I would squish up against each other on our favorite ride, where we would go around in a circle as the track carried us up and down in a wavelike motion. The speed and centrifugal force of the ride would result in the two of us mashed together, but even after many rides, I could never remember which side to sit on to avoid being the one smooshed against. In between going on rides, I gleefully watched my dad whack moles to win stuffed animals for us. Then he was off to shoot water into various targets. One of these was a shower curtain with the shadow of a buxom woman with a cap on her head, which, once successfully shot at, would drop down to reveal the image of a crusty old man standing in the tub. I think Dad hated that completely not-sexy old man, because he sometimes kept shooting water at him before moving on to other targets. I never tired of running around the amusement park, eating cotton candy, and screaming on the rides with my sisters and brothers. It was a luxury for us to all enjoy such an outing, but amusement parks were not so expensive back then.

There was a venue in town where we could go to watch wrestling matches on the weekends. When Dad wasn't out on his boat, he sometimes took us with him to watch the burly, sweaty men knock one another about in the ring. Most of the spectators were white men from around town. Their cheering, jeering, and grunting filled my ears and seeped into my head. They labored just like Dad, and it showed in their tanned skin, sun-bleached hair, coarse beards, and chapped faces. Cigarettes hung from their lips, bobbing up and down as they jumped or jerked about to cheer on their favorite wrestler. If I were my mother, I would have frowned upon Dad taking us to these matches. But I was six or seven years old, and I loved the excitement and the spectacle of the wrestlers' fighting and their theatrics in the ring. There was a great deal of slamming one another against the ropes, locking of heads as they pushed to and fro on the raised platform, and flexing of beefy arms and chest muscles. It was fantastic, so unlike the quiet life we lived in our housing project and the church that we went to on Sundays. We were heathens, just like the sun-weathered men around us and the burly wrestlers in the ring. I liked that we were part of the tapestry here, that we didn't stand out.

In his downtime, my father would *nhậu* with his buddies. Dad was a thin man of five foot seven who drank too much. Where Bruce Lee's slim body was strong and wiry as he bested opponents with his karate moves, my dad was simply an overworked fisherman who spent too much time on a wooden boat in the hot sun. Dad was too busy supporting seven kids and a wife to be happy, so he found happiness in beer bottles.

When it was his turn to host this crew of carousing men, Mom and the other wives prepared steamed rice, gourd soup, egg rolls, and salty meat dishes. My younger sister and I peeled the shrimp he brought home, leaving the tails on, and we would butter them before popping them into the little counter-top broiler in our kitchen. The men washed everything down with Miller Genuine Draft beer.

When his drinking mates made their way home and Dad was good and drunk, he would start in on my mom. I never knew what set him off, but he would hit her with his bare hands, striking her in the face, arms, and back. Maybe it was because she was fertile and had given him too many children. Maybe she had prepared the wrong soup. Maybe she had spent too much of his hard-earned money at the grocery store. Maybe she was just his punching bag, a place to strike against with all his anger and frustration for the endless fishing he did, the endless repairs he made, and the endless responsibilities he shouldered. One time, when she was learning how to drive, my mom scratched the car, having pulled up too close to the pole safeguarding the pump at the gas station. Maybe he hit her for that, too. I'll bet it was a relief to my mom when he died, and all that wailing she did at his funeral was set to her inner soundtrack, which probably sounded more like this: "Thank the Lord above, you are no longer of this world. I'm free from your abuse."

Not long after he died, she started hitting us kids. Maybe it was for all the times he had hit her. Maybe she was angry at us—seven unruly kids whom she now had to raise on her own. Maybe she blamed us for her aching head and weary body, the result of so much housework and worry.

Before he died, Dad often took us to the lake in a better neighborhood down the street from the government housing project that we lived in. We ran along the lake trail, chasing the ducks that called it home. Once we wore ourselves out, we would plunk down on the grass to rest and drink whatever water or soda we had thought to bring along. Ours was never an organized or grand affair. We sucked down our beverages while other families ate delicate sandwiches and sipped on juice from actual cups as they sat on comfortable picnic blankets.

It was also at this lake that Dad would search for the ducks' nests. He loved eating the eggs, but he loved even more eating the ducks themselves, which he would chase toward our car. When the birds were thoroughly spooked from his wild pursuing and gesturing, he would grab them by their necks and stuff them in pillowcases or rice sacks, which he conveniently carried with him. Into the trunk of the car they would go, and we could hear muffled flapping and quacking on the way home.

These were the ducks that ended up on the dining table when Dad caroused with his buddies. The ducks would be strung up, throats slit, and their blood drained and set aside to coagulate.

The meat was cooked, cubed, and topped with mint, roasted peanuts, and onions. All this was served in the reserved blood and presented in glass pie dishes. A squeeze of lime and eaten in a big slurp. Washed down with ice-cold beer. For us kids, it was washed down with beer if we were brave enough to try it, but more often, we gulped sweet, fizzy sodas to cut the tang of the blood and lime juice. It was not a proper *nhậu* unless there was duck blood pudding.

When I was in high school, living in the Midwest, far away from this chapter in my life, the thought of this duck blood concoction grossed me out, and I felt sorry for the ducks themselves. It was a wonder my dad never got in trouble for capturing them. I have never been able to look at a glass pie dish without seeing duck blood pudding in it. That really ruins my love of fruit pies.

The summer before he died, he must have felt his time was running short, because he went out and splurged on a stereo system, probably the only thing he ever bought for himself. There was an amplifier and a record player that went with the set. The speakers were these big, tall wooden boxes with soft, stretchy black fabric covers on the front, and they stood taller than most of us kids. "Don't ever put your hands on the speakers," Mom warned us after catching the little ones poking their tiny fingers into the covers. Her warning was as much for us as it was for herself, in case Dad decided it was her fault we ruined his speakers.

To minimize dust and in an effort to dress them up, Mom took some nearly sheer floral-print fabric and sewed covers for them. From those speakers, my dad blasted AC/DC, Journey, Boston, and Pink Floyd. He would put on a record, set the needle down, and slowly, so slowly, turn the volume knob until the music was loud enough for him to enjoy. The windows rattled and the knickknacks in the living room hopped their way along the shelves before falling over the edge. My mother must have hated that stereo system with every ounce of her being because it was a constant reminder of the money Dad wasted, never mind the volume-induced headaches. When he died, that stereo system, our black Ford LTD, and the boat he had just completed constituted the entire inventory of assets he left behind.

I remember examining his tanned, wrinkled face as he lay in his casket. He was a thirty-seven-year-old man with the face of a seventy-year-old, finally getting in that nap he always needed. I prayed to God that I would live to be forty because that would mean I had lived a good, long life.

Several months after he died, I woke up one night in the bed that I shared with Hà. Something had stirred me, and in the milky light that came from the lamppost outside, I thought I saw my dad's ghost floating above, watching over us. "Dad," I whispered, "is that you?" He didn't reply. "Will you come back to us? I miss you. Mom is selling your boat." Still no reply. "Will you always make sure we're OK? Will you make sure I'm OK?" He nodded and was gone.

Sometimes, when I'm praying, I speak to my dad. I pray to God, but there have been times I've directed questions and comments to Dad instead:

"Dad, we are moving to Kansas. We're not going to get to visit you anymore. Will you be lonely without us here?"

"Dad, please let me get this scholarship so that I can go to college. I want to go to college."

"Dad, give me the strength to finish this chemistry class. I hate it so much."

"Dad, what am I supposed to do with my life?"

"Dad, if law school is not for me, why am I here?"

"Dad, I think I've met the man I want to marry. Can you give me a sign that he's the one?"

"Dad, this baby I'm carrying is a boy, isn't it? Can you make sure he's beautiful and healthy?"

Speaking to him and asking him questions gave me the reassurance I needed to get through whatever was happening in my life. I'm not sure he would have had time or patience to give me advice if he were alive, but after his death, I found comfort in reaching out to him for the parental support and encouragement that I couldn't find with my mother.

I never directed anything about Mom to him. I figured there was no sense in him granting me any peace or guidance when it came to her, because he was so terrible to her when he was alive. I didn't even tell him when she got engaged to her second husband.

My Mother: Urban Farmer and the Queen's Mother

Before my mother became a widow and we moved to Kansas, she was an urban farmer. Our housing project was designed in a way that provided a good deal of green space between apartments. Where the buildings had their backs to one another, my mother and her neighbor friends used the land to garden. There were herbs—basil, mint, cilantro, and a horrible one that smelled like stinky fish. There were also bitter melons, bottle gourds, cucumbers, tomatoes, eggplants, chili peppers, and lettuces. My mother and her friends cultivated backyard gardens in the urban setting long before it was hip to do so. Miracle-Gro and heirloom seeds that were passed between the ladies resulted in a lush and thriving verdant landscape.

Once, when she ended up with more cilantro than we could eat and share, Mom bundled her fresh-picked herb and carried a box of it over to Piggly Wiggly, the grocery store across the street from our neighborhood. I went with her, curious to see what she was doing.

"I want speak your manager," she said to one of the workers

when we got to the produce section. The worker, not knowing what my mom wanted but also not wanting to have to deal with the Asian woman who spoke broken English, told us to wait and went into the back of the store. A few minutes later, a portly man in rust-colored slacks and a white short-sleeved button-up shirt and tie came out from the swinging double doors.

"May I help you, ma'am?" He looked at my mom and glanced down at me.

"You buy?" she asked him, holding out her box of cilantro. His brow crinkled in confusion. "You buy for me?" I understood that she meant *from*, not *for*, but I didn't speak up and just watched in fascination instead, curious to hear what he'd say.

"Uh, no, you buy from us," he said after a long pause, pointing from her to himself, still not quite understanding what was happening. Poor Mom and poor round-bellied man. This was not working.

I didn't know the English name of the plant at the time, so I couldn't help, but Mom was clever and made her way to the herb section in the chilled display case. We followed her over, and I spotted the sign above the herbs. *Cilantro*, it read. "She wants to know if you will buy this from her," I told him as I pointed to her box. "To sell here," I said as I pointed to the cilantro on display.

"Ooooohhhhhh," he said, stretching out the word as comprehension dawned. "Let me see what you've got."

He put a hand into the box and pushed the little bundles at the top aside to see the ones below, assessing their quality. He bent over, sticking his nose close to the cilantro, and inhaled.

"Well," he said, looking at me, "we don't normally buy from people off the street, but this looks really fresh and smells great. I'll take it."

I don't think I stood much higher than the worn-out brown leather belt around his waist. I watched his facial expressions, fascinated by this exchange in commerce that was happening between him and my mother. This was probably the first time

I ever saw someone selling something they had personally produced. He made an offer, and I turned to tell her she had a deal. I think it helped that he was familiar with us, having seen my family shop there.

The manager took the box from my mom and went to the back, returning about ten minutes later with some cash in his hand. My mom took the money, smiled, and thanked him, nodding a few times, as if to indicate she very much agreed with doing business with him, that this was the beginning of a beautiful and bountiful friendship, and we left. She smiled all the way home.

Back home again, my mom put away the money she had just made and went out to her garden to gaze at her enterprise. My mom had an entrepreneurial streak in her, even before she was widowed and needed it for survival. She was mentally assessing her situation, likely thinking, *What else could I sell?* I watched her from my position at the door, my back to the kitchen. The rows of herbs, vegetables, and hot peppers were straight, each plant in its spot in the raised soil. Bumblebees the size of pecans buzzed around from plant to plant. The Florida sun shone down on everything, and I remember the vibrant green of the leaves, the red of the ripe tomatoes hanging low on their vines, and the purple-flower-tipped basil plants against the backdrop of laundry drying on the lines, shirts, pants, and bedsheets fluttering gently when there was a breeze, kept in place with the help of wooden clothespins.

I don't think the manager intended to make a habit of buying from her, but she persisted in presenting him with such good produce that he was inclined to unburden her more often than not. In a time before food regulations could stymie her efforts, my mother was able to build a side hustle selling homegrown produce to our neighborhood grocer. Their arrangement ended when, a year or so after my dad died, we moved to a house across town that didn't have enough yard space for a garden.

Years later, and several states over, she would make and sell Vietnamese food to the local Asian supermarkets, continuing her entrepreneurial endeavors.

*   *   *

My mom spent most of her time cooking, cleaning, and doing laundry. Aside from her church group's community-service projects and her backyard garden, she had no free time for hobbies. This changed when my mom received a clipping of a Queen of the Night, a cactus plant, from a friend, around the time Dad died. The plant, her friend promised, would yield gorgeous, fragrant blooms as large as our faces once a year if she cared for it dearly. And she did.

The Queen of the Night became her one and only hobby that was just for her own pleasure. She volunteered at church and helped others, but she tended to that plant with more devotion than I ever knew her to care for anything else, including her garden. I envied the plant, its hallowed place on a little side table below the altar, situated on a delicate, cream-colored lace cloth underneath the ceramic pot that she planted it in after it had sprouted roots in a water glass.

The clipping was only about six or eight inches tall when it first moved in with us. At its peak, when I was in high school, the cactus grew so big that it occupied an entire corner of our living room. But before that, it was just a mere clipping, with unknown potential for grace, beauty, and devotion. *This* was her baby. We kids paled in comparison.

When her friend gave it to her, she promised Mom that in time, buds would appear and their stems would grow long, and from them, the most delicate white-petaled blossoms—edged underneath in pale pink, with buttery yellow stamens in the center—would reveal themselves slowly, only once a year, and only at night. Each blossom would fade before morning the

following day. I wondered why God would create such a flower
to exist for one night of glory. So much effort and beauty to shine
for so short a time. My mom loved plants and flowers, as demonstrated in her garden, but this cactus was not utilitarian. This
was purely a thing of beauty.

She watered it and watched over it. After it had been in the
pot of soil for several months, we noticed a little nub. The nub
grew into a tight blossom. Mom called her friends to share the
news: "It's going to flower!" I thought her heart would burst from
the joy she felt. I don't think she felt such unfettered happiness
with any of her pregnancies, but that's just petty me speaking.
I'm sure she anxiously awaited each and every one of us.

The weeks leading up to the big night were filled with regular check-ins, with Mom deciding whom to invite and what to
wear. She pestered us children to also decide what we would
wear, because though it wouldn't start opening until nearly 8:00
p.m., Mom was willing to allow us to stay up past our bedtime to
marvel at her miracle baby. The potted plant and the table it sat
on were pulled out, not just for better showcasing but also so that
the flower would have the room it needed as it bloomed.

On the night it was to blossom, wearing our Sunday best, we
sat and watched, with the camera and lots of rolls of film ready.
When we got bored, we wandered off to look for something to
eat or to play. It was a slow unfurling, and though it was neat
to watch, the early hours weren't much different from watching
grass grow or paint dry. My mom took photos throughout the
evening, but the best pictures were of the flower in full bloom.
Its subtle, sweet scent drifted around the room, carried in the air
around us as we moved back and forth. We posed standing next
to it, then sitting down, shifting positions to add or take away
individuals next to the flower.

Our childhood photo albums are filled with images of
this night-blooming cactus over the years. That plant was
one of us kids, except far more exceptional in its beauty and

accomplishments. It was the one child in the family who didn't disappoint, who didn't talk back. The cost of buying film and developing the images must have been great, but it was worth the joy the plant brought my mother.

I thought it was a silly diversion for her, but I can see now why my mother loved it so much. Her world was stressful and depressing, filled with kids constantly fighting, a drunk and abusive husband while he was alive, and the relentless demands of domestic life and making a living after he died. If she wasn't pregnant, she was caring for a baby. If she wasn't cooking, she was cleaning. I doubt there was a moment of quiet for her in that world. Her days and nights were filled with meeting the needs and demands of everyone around her. She never did anything for herself.

When this plant came into her life, she was newly widowed, overwhelmed, and worried that she might never gain her footing again, that every day forward would be a struggle. This plant was an opportunity for her to do something simple—and to do it because she wanted to, not because she had to. The cactus needed only a pot, some soil, a bit of water, and sunlight. Compared to everything else she was juggling, this was easy.

In my late twenties, after I moved to Hawaii, I came upon a variation of the cactus again. I was walking to a friend's house when I spotted it, my long-lost green sibling, except this time it was an overgrown and vast plant that covered a retaining wall made of lava rock bordering someone's front yard. I hadn't thought of my mother's Queen in years, had forgotten about all those late nights we'd spent together. And here it was, thriving in the warm and sunny climate of Hawaii.

I looked for blooms on this plant and found several of them in different stages of growth and decay. I laughed at the idea that my mother had coveted and cherished the plant as she did, because here was evidence that it was just as grown up as any of us kids. It was just as wild and free as I had become. I ran the tips of

my fingers against the smooth skin in the grooves, avoiding the
prickly bits along the raised edges. I closed my eyes and smelled
the fragrance of the wilted flowers that had bloomed in the night,
and it brought back memories of my mother's excitement, our
own excitement-turned-exasperation at her exuberance, and I
sighed. Before walking on, I whispered, "It's good to see you,
my long-forgotten sibling. I see you've grown up and done pretty
well for yourself." The thought had not occurred to me that this
particular cactus appeared to be blooming year-round, whereas
Mom's plant bloomed just once a year. Perhaps my green sibling
had been prickly in more than one way after all.

Mom's favorite child, her Queen of the Night cactus, 1985

These days, my mother has just a small bit of the original
plant left in her house, in a modest Chinese painted pot. She has
given away countless clippings of it over the years. Her friends
and acquaintances near and far who have received clippings have
shared pictures with her, their joy in the plant apparent in their
celebration of its annual blooms. I wonder how many of them

leaned on that cactus to get through bleak and lonely nights the way my mom did. It was deserving of the reverence that was bestowed upon it. Through a life of poverty, domestic abuse, death, and the struggle to survive, the Queen of the Night offered my mom something her children couldn't: a beautiful and simple moment of respite. It gave her joy.

Schoolyard Scuffle

My siblings and I all attended Archer Mills Elementary School in Panama City. As the third oldest, each fall, I would hear my new teacher say, "Oh, you're Hà and Cường's little sister." I liked that they knew my older siblings because that meant I wasn't just another student to them. My family was part of Archer Mills' history. Then our younger sister and brothers started school. As I escorted them to their classes each fall, I would hear their teachers mutter, "My goodness, just how many of you are there?"

I knew we were a large family, but it wasn't as if I could change that fact. Our next-door neighbors, the Phan family, had more than a dozen kids. Their school-aged children attended the same school as well. Two of the brothers even had names that all the teachers thought were the same. Chính and Chinh. The younger brother and I were the same age and in the same grade. Inevitably, our new teacher would ask, "Why did your parents give you and your older brother the same name?"

Each year, he would have to explain, "Our names sound different when you say them in Vietnamese." I could almost relate because Hồng and Hạnh sound similar, too, when westernized.

Fortunately, our names are spelled differently and sound completely different in Vietnamese.

Aside from us and the Phans, Archer Mills Elementary had a few other Vietnamese children among its population. We were mostly good students and did our best to stay out of trouble. We lined up quietly, placed our right hands over our hearts, and pledged allegiance to the US flag every morning, and we willingly ate our free school lunches. I especially enjoyed the fruit cocktail and spaghetti with meat sauce, and I didn't mind the carrot and raisin salad. We were refugee kids from Asia, but we sat among our white and Black classmates and were taught just as they were taught. This was before the education system evolved and accommodations were made for English-language learners.

Then, midway through fifth grade, Nga Trần happened.

Nga, her parents, and her two older siblings were newly arrived, landing in Florida after spending years in a refugee camp. They weren't Catholic, so we didn't know them from church, and I only ever saw her at school. Nga was two inches taller than me, but her frame was very thin compared to my pink and nourished body. Her big eyes gave her an innocent Puss in Boots look, though I often saw her squinting like Clint Eastwood in the midday sun, trying to appear tough. She walked like a cat, quiet and lithe, and constantly looked around, always at the ready in case a gunfight broke out. I was a tomboy, but she was more tomboy. I scored high on spelling tests, but she scored higher. I did well in math, but she did better. I think she spent a lot of time at home studying. Everything became a competition between us.

She refused to speak to me, except the one time she turned to me and said, "I hate you." Only it sounded like, "I het you." Message received, though. Hate me, hit me, het me. I knew what she meant.

After firing her warning shot, my new nemesis upped her game and started stealing my friends. Nga spread lies about me, causing a defection so significant, I became a pariah in the schoolyard. *She smell like she didn't take a bath for weeks. She share underwear with her sisters. She tattle on you with the teacher.* They were nonsense lies in her best English, not as good as my English, thank you very much, but her smear campaign worked because she was intimidating. Anyone who didn't join her ranks became her enemy.

I managed to keep two friends, sweet and soft-spoken Roy, an overgrown man-boy—he probably belonged in middle school—and Rachel, who lived with her mom across the street from our duplex in the housing project. The three of us hung out at the edge of the playground along the side of the red-brick school building. Nga and her newly acquired friends ruled the jungle gym. Among her gang were a set of triplets: Sabrina, Stephanie, and Susan. Big Black girls who were nice when they felt like it but hell when they decided otherwise, which was nearly all the time after Nga recruited them. The triplets hadn't been my friends B.N. (Before Nga), but we rode the same bus to and from school, so I knew them. Everyone knew them. Upon joining forces with their new leader, the triplets became trouble-makers and exuded an aura of menace. The rest of us knew to keep our distance.

"She's not very nice," Roy said one day in January as he glanced over to the jungle gym. He had been subjected to Nga's intimidation tactics but refused to denounce his friendship with me. Roy and I had been friends since first grade, and his loyalty meant a lot to me. Rachel became my friend in second grade when she moved into our housing project. She and I were BFFs.

"Yeah, tell me about it," I grumbled. We kicked the dirt and watched as Nga, the triplets, and a few other girls hung upside down on the jungle gym, talking and laughing.

Our new normal held until late March, when Nga strode up to me and said, "I gonna beat you up, and the triplets gonna help me." Her threat came from out of the blue. I had steered clear of her and the triplets and thought everything was fine.

I was scared witless. Fighting was not my jam at all. I spent the next few days avoiding them, hovering near teachers during recess, and running away anytime the girls approached me in the bathroom or hallway. It became increasingly difficult to keep my distance, however, especially on the bus.

"Tomorrow," Sabrina growled one afternoon as she and her sisters passed our seat, a few rows behind the driver. They squinted at me, then at Rachel, my seatmate. Three Clint Eastwoods in the big yellow school bus. They were spending too much time around Nga. A confrontation was imminent, and I was in danger of bodily harm. Scratch that. Rachel, who always sat with me on the bus, was also in danger of bodily harm. We held our breath until the triplets moved on and sat down two seats away. The triplets shifted closer and closer to our seat with each passing day.

"Oh my God, Rachel," I whispered. "What are we going to do?"

As soon as the bus pulled up to our street, Rachel and I bolted from the bus and sprinted for our respective homes. Later that evening, I met her on the roof of her house to brainstorm our way out of this fiasco.

"We could walk to school," she suggested. "I've been thinking about it. I've watched the road, and I know exactly how to get to school from here if we follow the path the bus takes."

"Won't that take forever?"

"Since we don't have all the pickups like the bus does, we'll get to school pretty fast. We may even get there before the bus." She was so confident in her assessment, I had no reason to doubt her. "Let's meet early—that way, we won't have to see the triplets."

I didn't tell my siblings or next-door neighbors that my life was being threatened; that was an obviously simple solution my scared fifth-grade mind failed to consider. The next morning, Rachel and I met twenty minutes before our usual bus pickup time and set off on foot, our school bags slung over our shoulders.

We passed the creek behind Rachel's house, turned right, and followed the road that ran alongside the woods. The weather was pleasant, and birds chirped in the trees. We crossed the bridge over the little stream where my mom had discovered snails, after which her love for Florida escargot took root. As Rachel and I cleared the bridge, our yellow school bus lumbered past, and we spotted the triplets' surprised looks in the back window. We reached the end of the street and crossed over to the left. We had been walking for twenty-five minutes.

"Maybe another five minutes, ten max. Just in time for school," Rachel assured me. I had never walked to school, so I trusted her estimate, but my feet were starting to blister. The bay ran along our right side, and I pointed out my dad's old boat dock in the distance. We marched on.

Twenty minutes later and very tardy, we arrived at school.

"My word! Why are you so late?" my teacher asked when I stepped inside the classroom. All eyes were on me, and as I surveyed the room, I spotted Nga in her seat, smirking at me and punching her right fist repeatedly into her left palm.

"I'm sorry, Ms. Jones. I walked to school today," I said before taking a seat.

"Did you miss the bus this morning, dear?"

"No, I just decided I'd walk."

Ms. Jones clucked and went back to taking attendance. I avoided eye contact with my nemesis as our teacher moved on to the morning's lessons. Roy was absent that day, and without his protection, Rachel and I hid in the far corner of the yard at recess. There was no avoiding evil Nga, however, and soon we were face to face with her as she came up to us, the triplets flanking her. Rachel and I looked at each other, and we knew it was time. We stood in between the lone tree and the chain-link fence as Nga made her approach with her gang of bruisers. There was nowhere to run. Years later, I watched *West Side Story* in my drama class, and it triggered my memory of this moment, causing me momentary stress.

"You gonna walk to school every day from now on? Like that's gonna keep you from getting beat up?"

I stood mute. I hadn't thought that far ahead, truth be told. I was already on the fence about walking home that afternoon because my feet were sore. Rachel, even less of a fighter than me, took a step back and retreated to the nearby tree. I couldn't blame her. This was between Nga and me. Rachel was caught in the crossfire of whatever this showdown was. I debated how to respond. What could I say to stop Nga from fighting me? What could I do?

"You think you're so tough," I squeaked out. "You don't scare me."

Nga wasn't your average movie villain. She didn't launch into a protracted speech about why she hated my guts so badly or how we had ended up here in this moment. She didn't waste time speaking on the finer points of schoolyard confrontations. Instead, she swiftly swung her right fist, and it immediately met my right eye. Thwack! I stumbled back.

It took a moment before the pain registered, and as soon as I felt it, I pressed my palm to my face and burst out crying. My right eye stung, and I imagined cartoon stars dancing around my head as I righted myself.

Susan, the smallest of the not-so-small triplets, high-fived her fearless leader. "Oh my God. That was awesome!" she exclaimed. Nga, with her bad-ass right hook, grinned.

"Let's go," she ordered. They stalked off, likely to return to their jungle gym.

Through my tears, I spotted our physical education coach monitoring the play structures and ran over to him.

"Mr. Thompson, Nga . . . punched . . . me . . . in . . . my . . .

face!" I could barely get the words out, I was so busy blubbering.

"What happened?" He wore his usual green polo tucked into tan khaki shorts and a whistle hung from the lanyard cord around his neck. There was no urgency in his query. He put both hands on his hips as he leaned forward to examine my face.

"Nga . . . she . . . hit . . . me, Mr. Thompson." I hiccupped.

"You look fine. Go to the girls' bathroom and wash your face." So much for garnering sympathy from the coach. Life was incredibly unfair!

Rachel, having emerged from behind the tree, caught up with me then, and Mr. Thompson allowed her to accompany me to the girls' bathroom. "Stupid Nga isn't even going to get in trouble!" I lamented as I washed my face and blotted my eyes with the scratchy brown paper towel. I was sure I'd have a black eye for days.

That afternoon, Rachel and I rode the bus home. It didn't occur to me until years later how dangerous it was that we had walked forty-five minutes to school that morning. We could have been abducted, hit by a car, or gotten lost. Anything could have happened.

Nga left me alone for the rest of the school year. I guess she was satisfied with her ambush, so she and the triplets called a truce. Maybe they didn't want to press their luck trying to fight me again. I was a wimp and posed no threat to them anyway. She didn't harass other students the way she had me. As an adult, I can understand her position. She'd spent years in a refugee camp in Asia, waiting to come to the United States, while I was presumably living comfortably in Florida. I had a head start on adjusting to my new life while hers was in limbo. She envied me, believing that my life was secure and carefree. She didn't know me at all. My dad had been dead for two years by then, and my mom struggled to keep us clothed and fed. As much as I appeared confident and settled, I wasn't the least bit of either. But what she saw as my Great American Life was what she wanted.

Grilled Cheese Fantasies

After nearly a year of my mom trying to keep our family afloat on her own, Aunt Kim Liên agreed to come down from Kansas to help us out. Aunt Kim Liên was a few years younger than Mom, the younger of my mom's two sisters. She was a nurse and had stayed behind in Việt Nam to care for our maternal grandfather when the rest of us left near the end of the war. By the time Aunt Kim Liên arrived in the United States after our grandfather died, she had some grasp of English and marketable skills, was single, and had no children. She was the perfect person to help out a grieving widow and overwhelmed mother of seven.

She and my mother opened a tailor shop, Kim's Alterations. They sold silk pajamas, belts in bright neon colors with butterfly buckles, and trinkets to supplement their income earned by way of thread and needle. Besides being a nurse, my aunt was also a skilled seamstress and could not only tailor and hem suits, but she once created a beaded wedding gown I was certain was fit for a princess. I marveled at her various talents and was happy to have her join our family.

Kim's Alterations was a tiny shop with two dressing rooms, tucked in between a sandwich shop and an insurance agency in a strip mall down the street from the city's main mall. In the days before my dad died, one of my school art projects, an Easter egg poster that I'd created with great care and many colors in crayon, had been hung up and displayed at the main mall. I was very proud of my accomplishment and begged my dad to take us there so that we could all admire my artwork. Diagonally across from that great mall was a large grocery store, and across a little field on the same side of the road was the strip mall where my mom and aunt worked their magic on dresses, shirts, and pants.

Not daring to restrict our income to just the alterations shop, my mom teamed up with her friend, who was also a neighbor of ours, to open a little take-out stand along the main drag by the beach. These were the days before Panama City and its beaches were thrust onto the college scene by MTV's spring-break exploits. While I refused to learn to work a sewing machine, I do remember putting in my time at the egg-roll stand. (Whether I was a productive contributor remains questionable.)

It was my first foray into customer service. We sold loads of egg rolls and, to go with them, two dips: a spicy Chinese mustard and my mom's homemade sweet-and-sour sauce. Her secret ingredient was applesauce; it created the perfect consistency and sweetness. For beachgoers who wanted something daring and spicy, we offered the mustard. Many times, my siblings, the neighbor kids, and I would hand out the little cups of mustard, then watch as unwitting customers generously dipped their egg rolls into the fiery sauce. Their faces would flush in horror as the heat of the mustard caught on their tongues and in their throats. We'd double over with laughter, ducking under the counter just inside the front window, having successfully pulled the same familiar prank on so many people. Over time, I think Mom's sweet-and-sour sauce became the preferred dip among our regulars.

I couldn't tell you how long my mom took part in the food stand; it may have been a few years, or it could've been just a couple of summers. The time eventually came for us to move on. I'd never known anything beyond Florida and Mississippi, where my dad's family lived and worked. We had taken a few family trips to Biloxi to visit aunts, uncles, cousins, and my dad's parents. My mom's family, on the other hand, had settled in the Midwest, so we moved to Kansas. Accustomed to lazy summers at the beach and the small-town life that we lived in Florida, I was devastated to learn we were moving to, in my mind, Nowhere. The idea that anything interesting existed in Kansas was laughable, and I swore to hate my mother (and Kansas) for the rest of my life.

* * *

The year before we moved to Kansas, I was in the seventh grade, and my friend Lynn convinced me to try out for the volleyball team. I was not athletic, and sports were not encouraged in our home, but I went along with Lynn, more out of curiosity than a desire to be on the team. I was the shortest of the dozens of girls who showed up, but somehow, I made the team. Perhaps the coaches felt sorry for me.

Proud for having earned the chance to play, I took it as an opportunity to challenge myself and to be part of a group working toward a common goal. Well, we were a misfit bunch of girls and couldn't quite get our act together. We didn't win a single game that season, but I treasured being a member of the team and playing among my friends. I was one of them in my volleyball uniform. I had imagined that sports were a very American concept, and being on the team meant that I had made it—I had achieved just the right balance between being Vietnamese and being American.

Ironically, what I remember most about playing volleyball isn't my feeling of belonging but how much grief my mother gave me for taking up her time when she had to pick me up from practice or after games. I would sit at the edge of the parking lot in front of the school, my eyes fixed on every car that passed along the road. Given that it would be late afternoon, there were very few cars in the lot, maybe four or five that belonged to teachers or the custodial staff. I would sit on the unyielding concrete curb for so long, my butt would grow numb.

One day, my mother pulled into the lot nearly half an hour late, and I was slow to get up.

"Get in," she growled as soon as I opened the door. She was abrupt, and her face was set in a frown. I'd hardly shut the door before we were on our way.

I imagined, in that moment, an entirely different conversation between us.

"Hi, honey," she'd say sweetly.

"Hi, Mom," I would reply. "Thanks for picking me up."

"Sorry I'm a minute late. I was busy finishing up dinner prep at home." Here, she would squeeze my shoulder gently and give me an apologetic smile and a shrug.

"It's OK, Mom. I know you're busy and you work hard." I'd be incredibly wise in my twelfth year of life, knowing my mother's struggles, her strain at raising seven children on her own.

"How was volleyball? Did you guys win?" She'd always want to know how our team played. I had watched too much *Leave It to Beaver*; my fantasy version of my mom was the saccharine June Cleaver in her full-skirted, tea-length dress.

"Oh, we were not so great and we didn't win, but I had fun," I'd tell her.

"I'm so glad you're enjoying the volleyball team," she'd say, adding, "and I'm so proud of you for really giving sports a try. I wish I could actually be there for your games." Fifties mom but with modern views on girls and sports, of course.

"Thanks for your support, Mom. I know you can't make it to my games, but I appreciate that you pick me up after."

Instead of that loving, encouraging conversation, however,

we sat in silence as my downtrodden mother navigated her way from my junior high school to our townhouse ten minutes away. At least silence was better than whatever else she might decide to say about my sport, my appearance, or my performance.

I had lots of imaginary conversations like this with my mom when I was younger. They fed my hunger for a mother who was capable of hugging, smiling, and laughing. They painted a picture of a mother who didn't have to work so hard to feed and clothe her seven kids. They allowed me to have an open, loving, and supportive dialogue with a woman I knew was incredibly strong, yet utterly overwhelmed and flawed in her attempt at motherhood.

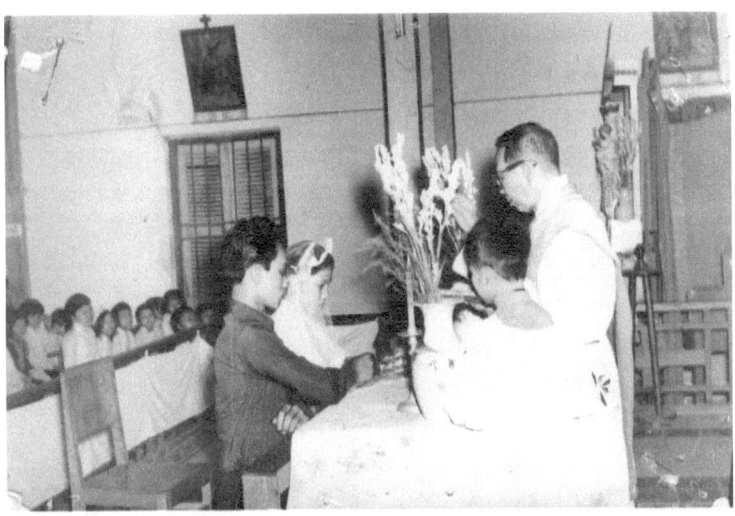

Mom and Dad's Catholic Church wedding, 1964

It was silly, really, for me to want a mother who would hug me and smile with joy, because that just wasn't in her nature at the time. She smiles more these days, in retirement, but in my childhood, my mom was too busy cooking, mending and sewing at the shop, and cleaning around the house—basically, doing what she knew to earn an income. She never gave a thought to what she wanted or needed. Tending to herself was not part of her childhood and had never been part of her adult life. She and my father were married by their parents' arrangement when they were still teenagers, and in the sepia-tone wedding photo that they managed to leave Việt Nam with, I saw only a solemn couple embarking on a lifelong journey of imposed togetherness.

* * *

With hardly any English-language skills to her credit, my mother somehow managed to balance government help with her own meager earnings to keep us housed, clothed, and fed. One way that the government helped was through food stamps, which featured coupon books valued in ones, fives, and tens that she used to buy groceries. The coupons valued at one dollar were printed in a milk-chocolate-brown ink, the image of America's founding fathers signing the Declaration of Independence to the side. The paper itself was not smooth, like regular paper, but softer, like fabric.

It wasn't until I was nearly a teenager that I began to really understand the government program behind those coupon booklets and what they meant. The booklets revealed to the cashiers who rang up our groceries, and all the customers in line behind us, that we were poor. I stopped standing with my mom at the checkout, wandering just far enough away to pretend I wasn't with her. And if she asked me to run to the store to buy something for her, I barely looked up at those around me when I went to pay, feelings of shame and embarrassment swallowing me whole. I hated that we didn't have real money to spend.

Just as I imagined the cozy and loving June Cleaver conversations with my mother, I often imagined that we lived in abundance. One of the most infuriating phrases of my childhood in response to "Is there anything to eat?" was my mom's reply, "Just eat whatever's there to get you by." It was as if even she knew that what she brought home wasn't anything that would hit the spot. As an adult, I eat conscientiously, and I savor what I eat, no matter what it is. I don't eat *just to get by.*

Mom brought home bags and bags full of fruits, vegetables, rice, bread, milk, and cereal, but they never had anything I really wanted—never anything my non-Vietnamese classmates were enjoying. I remember the government-issued blocks of cheddar cheese that must've weighed five pounds each. I longed for the individually wrapped Kraft Singles American instead. I dreamed of gooey grilled cheese sandwiches featuring at least two slices of Singles, fresh out of their plastic wrap, melted to perfection between two pieces of buttered white bread, hot from the griddle. The government cheddar just didn't melt the same way.

I remember the Total cereal that my siblings and I would eat with several teaspoons of sugar. We desperately wanted Corn Pops, Alpha-Bits, and Honey Smacks, the sweet cereals that were too expensive for our family's meager budget. The food stamps program required us to buy only the healthy stuff, so Total was what we got. It has been decades since I've had it, and I could live the rest of my life without another bowl.

"There's nothing good to eat!" my siblings and I would lament. Our mother must have hated how often we complained about food.

In my food fantasies, I imagined my classmates eating amazing and delectable feasts, filled with peanut butter and jelly, fried bologna, and ham and cheese sandwiches. (I guess I had a serious thing for sandwiches.) My classmates ate at tables that overflowed with fried chicken and fluffy mashed potatoes in pools of the richest brown gravy. Extra-cheesy pizzas and big juicy burgers were piled high, alongside crisp, salted French fries. My classmates were living in food heaven.

* * *

I sometimes wonder how my mother didn't go crazy raising seven kids, but then I think that perhaps she did. She berated us—nothing was ever good enough—and she whipped us to keep us in line. Hers was not the life she ever wanted or imagined she would live.

One day during high school, report cards were sent home.

"Where's the other A?" my mother asked, looking across the room at me.

I was standing in the entrance to our living room, having just come home from school. My mother was sitting on the dark-brown, shimmery velour sectional sofa, my report card in her dry, calloused hands. I couldn't see the cigarette burn hole from where I stood, but I knew it wasn't far from where she sat. Mom was a smoker. The living room walls were finished in a rough texture, painted off-white but with dark-orange accents in the nooks and crannies. I hated that wall because if we accidentally rubbed up or fell against it, it would scratch our skin and snag our clothes.

"Well?" She wasn't having any of my delay tactics.

"I have six As," I finally said to her. I knew what my grades were. My teachers had told me, each of them congratulating me for a great semester.

"But you don't have all As," she retorted.

"Is that all you care about? That I get all As? I get one B, and the rest of it means nothing?"

The more questions I asked, the shakier my voice got. I could feel hot tears threatening to fall. I had worked so hard for these grades. I struggled in my math and science classes, never mind what people said about Asians being brilliant in those subjects.

"You're going to cry now?" She spat the words at me in disgust. She hated when her children cried. We were weak when we cried. When she beat us, if we cried, she would hit harder.

"What are tears going to do for you? You think crying is going to earn you that A you didn't get?"

"Can't you just be happy that I got six As? Do you know that a B is still a good grade?"

I was close to finishing high school at this point, and despite my mother's firm belief that I would attend Wichita State University, I had secretly resolved to move out and go away for college. My escape was imminent, and I could taste freedom. Screw her bullshit expectations. I was feeling bolder; my exhaustion from her relentless displeasure was giving way to a renewed energy to fight back. To fight against her.

"You're going to speak to your mother like that?"

"Yes, I am going to speak to you like this. Why shouldn't I? You don't care about me. You care about me getting all As so that you can brag to your friends."

She started to stir from her seated position on the couch.

"You know what, Mom? I got six As and one B. That's good enough for me. In fact, that's more than good enough. It's not my problem that it's not good enough for you."

Before I lost my courage, I ran down the hall to my bedroom, grabbed my work uniform from the closet, and stormed out the front door. Work was my escape. I had started working at the age of fourteen, and in high school, I spent most evenings, weekends, and holidays at Tippin's Restaurant and Pie Pantry. There, I could be the phenomenal cashier and hostess that I was and pretend my mother was not verbally and physically wearing me down. I soaked up the praise from my managers and coworkers, smiled at customers coming and going, and didn't have to deal with my immigrant mother's anger.

In my beige uniform, I wasn't an awkward Việt American girl. I wasn't a victim of life's circumstances. At Tippin's, I set aside my longing to be somewhere else, to be someone else, because it gave me a safe place to do a good job and get paid for it. I could feel the potential of whatever I might choose to do for a living as an adult when I counted out the change to customers. I could feel the opportunities that were going to open up after high

school. I just had to be patient. In the meantime, Tippin's was a
place that made me feel normal, where I was valued, and where
my missing A was inconsequential.

I never talked to my mom about my grades after that, and
when she brought up the subject, I would change topics. It in-
furiated me that she fixated on the missing seventh A instead of
being proud of me for the six As I did earn. It was hard living
with a mother for whom nothing was ever good enough. Yet,
despite hating her constant criticism, I ended up being hard on
myself. An entire childhood with her conditioned me to believe
that I had to be the best, or I was nothing at all. It would take me
years of being away from her to begin shedding the weight of
her high expectations and forgive myself for the mistakes I made
along the way.

Friendships Are Like
Butter, Rice with Butter

My mom never liked that my siblings and I had friends. She didn't understand why we needed them and actively discouraged us from developing or maintaining friendships. She never explained to us where her views on friendship came from. I could only speculate that she must not have had any friends growing up. Maybe there had been no one for her to confide in, no one to share jokes with. She must have had little joy and laughter when she was young—otherwise, why would she prohibit us from having any in our lives?

I desperately wanted to have friends and be invited to their birthday parties and sleepovers. My siblings and I had cousins on my dad's side of the family living in the same city, and we played with them often, but we inevitably made friends with classmates and kids in our neighborhood. Having American friends made me American, too.

When I was in the sixth grade, my mom finally agreed to let me host one of those coveted sleepovers. I don't know whether she had temporarily eased up on her anti-friendship campaign or if I was particularly well behaved that week, but I welcomed the opportunity with a great deal of glee. Finally! A friend was coming over to spend the night. It was going to be the best sleepover ever.

My friend Rachel and I played games and told stories in the bedroom I shared with my sisters. When it was time for dinner, we crowded around the table, and Rachel, a chubby white girl with blonde hair, squeezed in beside me. Mom had made gourd soup, salty fried pork belly, and sautéed greens, all to be enjoyed with rice. Rachel took one look at the bounty before us and said, "Can I have just rice?"

I translated for my mom, and she shrugged and said, "If that's all she wants."

With her little bowl of plain rice in hand, Rachel looked at me and asked, "Could I have salt and butter on it?"

I could only look at her, horrified. *Oh my gosh.* Rice was meant as a neutral base for all the other flavorful dishes of meats, vegetables, and soup that made up a proper meal. Why would anyone ruin rice by putting salt and butter on it? It sounded wrong.

"She wants salt and butter," I finally said in Vietnamese to my mom. My siblings snickered, furthering my horror. I thought this girl was my friend. Someone I knew well. We had been friends since second grade. I didn't know her at all, apparently.

Mom's response was swift. "Who eats rice with butter?" And instead of stopping there, she added, "What's wrong with white people?" Rachel didn't need to understand Vietnamese to know what she said. My mortification was complete.

After another minute of my mom's tirade against white people's sacrilegious ways with rice, my poor friend got her spoon of margarine (we didn't have butter back then, as it cost more) and some salt. She didn't have more than one bowl of rice before we went off to bed, too afraid to ask for more salt and "butter."

I'm certain Rachel fell asleep hungry that night because, in the dark room, her stomach grumbled its displeasure.

I never got invited to her house for a sleepover, and Rachel never asked to come to my house again. It must have been so awkward for her to be surrounded by my brothers and sisters and my mom, all of us staring at her in disbelief as she ate her buttered, salted rice. Even if we hadn't been staring at her, she couldn't eat in peace because my mother muttered under her breath between bites of her salted pork and greens for the duration of the meal.

It was such a shame I never got the chance to spend the night at her house. If Rachel had invited me, I would have gotten the chance to eat spaghetti, hamburgers, hot dogs, and pizza. I was sure I had missed a prime opportunity to live like a real American. Because that's what white people eat, right? When they're not eating rice with salt and butter, of course. As much as I daydreamed about what she ate at home, I stubbornly chose to set aside this incident, not wanting to see her way of eating rice as truly a bad thing. I still wanted to be like Rachel. To be her.

On occasion, my mom would remind me of the time I had invited the white girl over, but I refused to let her ribbings get to me. For her, having friends was not just a waste of time—having white friends was just outright silly. White people didn't understand us. They ate different things. In fact, they did everything differently.

*   *   *

I started ninth grade when my family moved to Wichita, Kansas. At Jardine Junior High School, I suffered the shock of learning about newly arrived Southeast Asian refugees and their journeys to America. Until I met the Vietnamese, Laotian, and Cambodian students at Jardine, I had never heard of Laos or Cambodia. I had no idea that hundreds of thousands of Vietnamese refugees were still coming to the United States. Very timidly, I formed friendships with a few of the Southeast Asian students.

I ended up being friends with a sweet and quiet girl named Bé (but we called her "Bee") Nguyễn. I was sure my mom would be OK with Bé, given that she was a smart Vietnamese girl. I liked Bé because she worked hard to learn English, and nothing deterred her from being an honor-roll student. But the truth was, she also made me feel more American. She was new to the United States, and I was well assimilated and wiser than she to American ways.

"I saw a sign the other day that said *Yard Sale*," Bé said to me one day.

"Yeah?" I replied. I wasn't sure where she was going with this.

"Well," she said, "how do the buyers remove the yard once they buy it?" It took me a moment to understand what she was asking, and I laughed at her confusion. I explained to Bé what yard sales were and went on to describe garage sales for good measure.

Bé and I sat next to one another in English as a second language (ESL) class and passed notes back and forth, so it was natural that we wanted to pair up for projects. One class project required us to get together outside of school. Poor Bé had suffered through the chicken pox just before she came to my house to get our project done; her face was marked with leftover spots.

My mom took one look at her and blurted out, "What happened to you?"

Not, "Hello, welcome to our home."

Not, "Hello, and what is your name?"

Not, "Hello, how are you?"

My mother had no filter.

"I was sick with chicken pox," Bé said to her quietly.

"Oh my God, Bé, let's go." I was humiliated that my friend was being treated poorly by my mom and quickly ushered her into my bedroom so that we could get started on our school project. With my mother's track record for belittling my friendships and friends, Bé was thereafter forever known as "Chicken Pox Girl" anytime my mom asked about her or felt like making fun of her.

Chicken Pox Girl is probably a medical doctor now. I like to think Bé proved that she was better than the stupid name my mom gave her. My white friends couldn't pass Mom's rice-eating test, and my Vietnamese friends were defined by their exposure to contagious diseases. There was no winning on the friendship front.

*   *   *

The secret I kept from my friends until I was nearly out of high school was the fact that my mother beat my siblings and me. From the outside, no one would have guessed that my mother physically abused us. She was a pro at managing a public profile that was nothing like her personal one. She was the gentle mother and role model to lots of kids in our community, and she devoted a great deal of her free time volunteering in various church activities. I squirmed every time one of my friends or a member of our church's youth group expressed how much they wished my mom was theirs. *You can have her,* I thought. *If only you knew.*

In the privacy of our home, Mom would be in the middle of whipping my siblings and me with thin switches she fashioned from branches off the tree in our backyard. "You kids are so disobedient!" she would snarl at us. We may have forgotten to pick up our toys. We may have made a mess in the kitchen. We may have played outside too long. Every little thing would set her off. Then, the telephone would ring, and the devil that was in front of us would turn into a saint as she answered with a singsong voice, "Hellooo?" The caller might have thought my mother was just enjoying a fine joke when the phone rang, not whipping her unruly kids.

She would then proceed with the lightest, fluffiest conversation with whoever was on the other end. Never mind that we were still kneeling on the floor (on top of shoes, if we were particularly wretched) in the living room, defeated little ducks all lined up in a row. We served time in our little hell while our mother was sweet as cotton candy in the kitchen.

"Oh, so-and-so, it's you! I'm so glad you called." She would fall into the conversation with someone from church as if there weren't any pressing matters to tend to. Her voice was like the song of a happy bird, chirping away as if, just the moment before, she was not calling up welts and bruises, breaking the skin on her own children with her whip.

In those conversations, I saw the glaring difference in how she operated at home and in public. I saw how good she was at making people believe her to be the perfect example of motherhood. But in my young mind, I never thought to wonder if other parents were doing the same. Were my friends punished the way I was punished? Did they cover their legs in long pants in the middle of summer because they had to hide the purple, green, and yellow bruises in differing stages of healing that they got from their mom or dad? Was this style of parenting just another thing about being Vietnamese or Asian to be ashamed of?

It's hard to sit here as an adult and reflect back on my mother's abuse when, from her point of view, she was being the best parent she could be, disciplining us as she saw fit with the parenting skills she had learned from her own parents. A smack on the bum sends a message and toughens up kids for adult challenges; heaping praise on them all the time doesn't.

I accepted what my mom did, though, even if I never felt we were so horrible that we needed to be physically punished. Not that one time when my brothers played with matches and accidentally set the bedroom closet on fire, though they were being reckless. Not the time I pushed my brother Tiến too hard on the swing at the playground and he fell off, breaking his arm. Not when I was frustrated with my mom and hung up the phone on her, though I was disrespectful and childish. It was just her way of raising us.

So what if I stole something from the nearby Zayre discount store? It was a little globe that doubled as a piggy bank, and I was desperate for it. "Can we get this?" I had asked my mom at the store. "No, we don't have money for that." I carried it around the store casually and walked confidently through the checkout line with it. *If I act like we've paid for it, no one will notice.*

"We will all go to jail for your crime!" Mom lamented when she caught me with it after we got home. I didn't think I had a future in shoplifting, but to Mom, our childhood exploits meant we would end up as miscreants or criminals. I got spanked for it, but I cherished my stolen piggy-bank globe for years.

During my senior year of high school, I confided in Kate, a classmate of mine, giving her a glimpse of the bruises on my legs. I don't know why I finally gave away my family's secret. It must have been a particularly trying week with my mother.

I told Kate my mother beat me. "Why don't you call the police?" she asked. The idea had crossed my mind dozens of times over the course of my childhood, but when Kate asked, my answer was immediate. "They'll arrest her and take us away. I don't want that."

I had accepted that although my mother beat us, the beatings were better than being put in foster care and having her in jail. It was better than living on the streets. She was a single parent. We were seven kids. She barely spoke English and did what she had to do to support us. She put food on the table by cleaning houses in the nice part of town, and she kept us from straying too far out of her reach by beating us. We lived in fear. Fear of her. Fear of the world at large. But without a clear, safe alternative, it was better to keep things as they were.

After that revelation, I begged Kate to keep my secret. Then I avoided her, afraid that she would tell our teachers or counselors about the abuse. I convinced myself that if I kept a low profile, she would think of it no more. Kate wasn't a friend who would tell other students, but I dreaded being hauled away by social workers at any moment. We didn't keep in touch after graduation, and I was fine with that. I hoped that she had forgotten about me.

My brother Tiến shared a meme on social media last year. A white mother and son are arguing. She is pointing her finger at him while he appears to be yelling at her. Just below that image is a photo of Rocky Balboa, with both eyes swollen nearly shut and his cheeks freshly bruised. The caption read: "Me after talking back to my mom in 1985." Below the post were fifty "Likes" and many laugh emojis, with comments from friends that included images of a long feather duster and a gleeful, "Truth!"

I struggled for decades with the way my mom disciplined me as a kid, but apparently, others, my brother included, were able to reflect on their childhoods and revel in having been on the receiving end of corporal punishment. To me, it's a strange thing to joke and laugh about. I hate that my mom beat me, and I don't find it the least bit funny.

Such Incivility, Dishonesty, and Thievery!

When we moved to Kansas, we rented a three-bedroom apartment in a large complex across the field from a trailer park in south Wichita. It wasn't the tony side of town, but this was after our time in public housing projects, so it was high living, even if it meant eight of us had to share tight quarters.

This was our first foray into living less among Vietnamese refugees and more among regular American folks. We played in the open space behind the complex, and my brothers made friends with some boys in the trailer park next door. Our initial transition wasn't so bad, and it seemed that life in middle America wasn't going to be the tragedy I thought it would be.

Then we met our next-door neighbors. They seemed perfectly normal. They were a family with three little kids who played in the parking lot and vacant field, just the same as we did. We weren't overly friendly, but we were civil and said hi when we saw them.

We must have lived there for a few months before our mail started going missing. It wasn't the letters and bills that were

disappearing. Packages my mom was expecting were not showing up. Boxes of clothes, herbal medicine, and Asian sundries of
no significance to anyone but us were shipped yet never delivered. "Didn't you send the stuff?" Mom would ask her friends
over the telephone. "Yes, weeks ago!" they would reply.

My siblings and I suspected the culprits were our neighbors.
We started our own little investigative scheme to flush them out.
"Let's box up some random junk for them to steal," my brother
Cường suggested. We put out a couple of small boxes filled with
rocks, broken toys, and papers when we knew our neighbors
would be arriving home. Then we stationed ourselves inside,
and Cường watched through the peephole in the door. "What's
going on out there?" I whispered. It didn't take long. "Just as we
suspected!" Cường exclaimed. "Those jerks just took our fake
mail!"

I was bewildered. Such incivility, dishonesty, and thievery!
We were all poor people in this apartment complex. What was
there to steal? After solving our case, I never bothered to speak
to them again. But I'm sure they never noticed me or my resolve
to give them the cold shoulder. After all, I was just some teen-
aged kid living next door to them.

A few months after this spate of thievery, we neared the end
of our lease, and my mom wanted my older sister, Hà, and me to
find us a house to rent. We were crammed into the small apartment space and were in desperate need of room to spread out.
A house with a yard would do. My older sister could pose as an
adult, and I was well spoken enough to call and inquire about
rental listings in the newspaper. We tackled the classifieds with
gusto, calling agents and landlords in more desirable neighbor-
hoods. "What about this one?" I would ask Hà each time I came
across a promising description of a house.

Having lived in the United States nearly all my life, I spoke
English just as well as any born and bred American kid (even
though I was labeled ESL by my middle school teachers). On the

phone, I sounded like a native English speaker, but I was new to finding a place to live.

"Hi, uh, I, uh, I'm, uh, calling about the house you have for rent?"

"Which one? I have several houses listed in the paper," the lady on the other end replied. My palms were sweating.

"Oh, I didn't know. Um, the one on Murdock. Is it, uh, available still?"

"Look, honey, you sound very young. Is this a joke? Do your parents know you're on the phone?"

I needed to up my game. Through a few more calls like that, I perfected my list of questions and took on a more confident tone.

"Good morning. I am interested in the house you have for rent on North Ohio Avenue."

"Mmm. That's a nice house. Just listed for rent."

"It's still available? Terrific!" I did my best adult-sounding voice. "I would be so pleased to see it as soon as possible. But before we settle on a time, I'd like to find out more about the house."

"Yes, of course. What would you like to know?"

Excellent. "What is the total square footage? Is there a laundry room? And how many parking spots come with the place?" I went down my list, jotting down answers as I went.

We didn't manage to see very many houses, but when we found one we wanted to rent, I helped my mom fill out the rental application, and we submitted it. After a few days, we'd had no word from the landlord, so I called her. "Hello, Ms. Jean, this is Hong. My mom and I saw the house on Harrison on Monday."

"Hmm, yes, what can I do for you?" Ms. Jean replied curtly. My heart sank just a little.

"Well, we were hoping you had good news for us. We really liked the house and feel it's exactly what we're looking for," I said cheerily, hoping to turn things around.

"Oh, no, I'm sorry dear, your application was denied," she responded.

I took a breath to calm myself. "May I know why our application was denied?"

"Well, we can't rent to troublemakers who steal mail," she said.

"Who told you that? We aren't troublemakers! We haven't stolen anything!"

"Your current manager told me that. She informed me that you've not been good tenants. I'm sorry, but I won't rent to you. Good luck with your search." She hung up before I could say anything else.

I was livid and immediately marched over to speak to our apartment manager, Kathy, an older lady taller than me by several inches, her hair in big curls, with long bangs rounded over her forehead.

"Why did you say that we are troublemakers and mail thieves?" I screamed as soon as I walked in. I had caught her by surprise; it took her a few seconds to register what I had said.

"That is no way to speak to an adult," she replied, avoiding my question. I had worked myself into such a fury that I burst into tears. She watched me from behind her desk. I stood just inside the door, crying, for a few minutes.

When I finally calmed down enough to speak, I said, "We have never stolen anyone's mail. Our neighbors have been the ones stealing packages from our door. My brothers and sisters and I play in the back. We don't bother anyone. You've been completely unfair in your judgment of us, and now we cannot find a house."

"But your neighbors told me that your family has been stealing their mail," she said, but it sounded more like she was trying to convince herself.

"Well, they're lying, and they were probably afraid we were going to rat on *them*."

I elaborated, but she was unmoved. When it became clear that justice was not going to be served that day, I left feeling shattered.

We eventually moved into a house that Uncle Tuyền helped my mom find. I lived in that house until I left for college, but the revelation that such horrible people occupied this earth set within me the conviction to never be a victim again. I vowed then that I would get a proper education and fight for myself as best I could, shitty people of the world be damned.

Underdogs

Two of the most significant revelations I had when we moved to Kansas were discovering that (1) there were other Asians in America and (2) many of them had been part of the American patchwork before the influx of Vietnamese and other Southeast Asian (collectively referred to as Indochinese) refugees that began in the 1970s. I'm not sure how or why this information was never imparted to me, but in my small world, I took for granted that most Asians were Vietnamese and that we had all arrived at the end of a terrible war that tore apart our home country.

In Florida, I had made friends with only white and Black Americans, and any exposure I had to Asians was restricted to my cousins and the families of our insular Catholic community. It was a very straightforward existence, given that I learned to categorize those around me as white, Black, or Vietnamese. When we moved to Kansas and I started ninth grade at Jardine Junior High, I found myself in the company of students from Laos, Cambodia, China, and Japan. What a complete shock to meet kids from other countries who may or may not have gone through what my own family had experienced.

To say that I fell in with the Asian crowd in middle school

is slightly misleading because the school's population was so heavily skewed that way, I could not help but mix and mingle with my Asian counterparts. Jardine was located down the street from a government housing project where most of the residents were recently arrived refugees from Southeast Asia.

Having spent most of my own life in the United States, I spoke English better than I spoke Vietnamese, and in Florida, I had never been in ESL. In fact, the school system in Florida did little to distinguish nonnative English speakers from the rest of the student body. Until we moved to Wichita, I was taught English alongside other students, with no deference or leniency I could discern, and I had mastered my adopted language as well as or better than those around me.

The school administrators in Kansas tested my English-language abilities when I was first enrolled, and they were astonished to find that I fell within the 98th percentile. My language skills were well above those of the school's Asian students. Instead of placing me in regular English classes and leaving it at that, however, they decided that my language skills would serve to boost the other students.

"We believe you'll really motivate your classmates when they hear you speak." They made it sound like such an honor that it did not occur to me to refuse being placed in ESL. I was a peer, strikingly similar in appearance, someone my cohorts could strive to emulate. For the entire school year, I found myself sitting in two long hours per day of ESL, learning how to diagram sentences and regurgitate homonyms. We engaged in spelling contests and countless other games to increase our knowledge of English syntax and American colloquialisms. I could say it was torture, especially the day I couldn't remember how to spell the word *dizzy* during a spelling round-robin (I'll never live that down); in truth, ESL class was probably where I learned to really love English and recognize its value. I believed English was my ticket to bigger and better things in life.

Despite being positioned as a beacon of hope and English fluency, I felt quite lost among my classmates when I tried to relate to them. I discovered right away that I didn't know enough Vietnamese to keep up with their lively discourse in the schoolyard. Over the years, adamant that we would learn to read and write in Vietnamese, Mom had sent us to after-school classes at the church in Florida and to summer programs she found when we arrived in Wichita. I wondered when I would ever need Vietnamese as an adult and felt it was a waste of time to learn a language that belonged to a tiny little country I couldn't remember and had no plans to visit.

Confronted by my Vietnamese classmates, though, I began to wish I had applied myself. "If you're Vietnamese, why can't you speak it better?" I was asked that a few times. Their question wasn't meant to be malicious or derisive; they were genuinely curious to know why I couldn't keep up with them. I primarily spoke the language within my family, but my fluency was challenged by these ninth-grade recess and lunch conversations. The speed with which I processed the words and spoke was much slower than theirs. Unable to maintain their fast-paced banter, I reverted to English all the time.

The administrators had another brilliant idea. "We believe your classmates would really appreciate your guidance." I was appointed to serve as a peer counselor to my classmates, and a few times a week, I sat with them one on one. In their emerging English, they related their worries, struggles, and histories. They had maturity and wisdom from tough life experiences that I couldn't relate to. They knew hunger, fear, and sadness unlike anything I had lived through. The most tragic event in my own life had been my father's death, but nearly five years had passed, so the pain of it had faded. I responded with what I felt were sage bits of advice about how to overcome these obstacles and concerns, but in my own mind, I wondered how I was ever put in such a weighty role. I was convinced that I lacked the necessary skills and knowledge to make any difference.

One day, a cute and popular Vietnamese boy in my class approached me with a note. It read, "Do you want to be my girlfriend? Yes/No." There were two boxes, one next to each response. I was to check the box reflecting my preference. I checked yes, then spent the entire lunch period holed up in the girls' bathroom, hiding from my new boyfriend. I felt my naiveté keenly as he and his friends stood in the hallway calling my name. News spread across the schoolyard, and other students began to congregate in the doorway, beckoning me to reveal myself. I waited until long after the bell rang, signaling an end to lunchtime, before I dared to reappear and slink along the quiet corridor to my next class. I had effectively destroyed my exalted reputation as a worldly and brilliant girl with my show of cowardice and innocence. Embarrassed, I did my best to avoid him for the remainder of the school year.

*   *   *

Jardine was the only school I went to where I found myself surrounded by so many Asians, particularly students from Cambodia, Laos, and Việt Nam. My family lived many miles away in an apartment complex where most tenants were non-Asian. Church was the only other place where I would interact with other Asians. Because of where we lived, when I graduated from Jardine, I went to a different high school than my middle school classmates and returned to befriending mostly non-Asians. My shift was not because there weren't Asians at my high school. Rather, I had begun to slowly drift away from church activities and divorce myself from those who looked like me and whose histories were similar to my own. From tenth grade on, I was drawn to fellow underdogs of other nationalities instead. I felt a kinship to them; we didn't fit in with the athletes, punks, or preppy kids. My high school friends were Lebanese, Egyptian, Hispanic, and a few white students I knew from drama. If I couldn't be white, I would at least pretend I wasn't Vietnamese.

I did have two Asian friends in high school, but we rarely spoke of race and ethnicity. Juliette was mixed race; her mother was Filipina and her father was white. We goofed around and cruised the main street downtown on the weekends (her parents following behind to keep a watchful eye on us), but we never spoke about her being mixed race or me being Vietnamese. Then there was Kari, who was Vietnamese and lived nearby. Like Juliette and with all my other friends, I saw us as having different backgrounds because Kari was a Buddhist from Central Việt Nam. The other Vietnamese students in our school were friends with one another, but I was an outsider by choice, always nodding to them in acknowledgment, never jumping in to join their group.

It wasn't until I was in law school nearly two decades later that I found a true Asian friend in a Filipina gal in my contracts class. Abby and I were together so much of the time that our classmates referred to us as two peas in a pod. By that time, I had started to travel more and sought out relationships based on shared interests, not a personal agenda. I learned more about other Asian cultures through people I met and grew to appreciate their chapters within American history. Abby was my maid of honor when I got married many years later.

I was well into my twenties before I understood what it means to be Asian in America, and that delay in acceptance and awareness astonishes me. Instead of devoting time to hiding my Vietnamese heritage, I was finally embracing and sharing it. I was slowly recognizing that we are all human, no matter where we're from and what we've been through; there's no shame in being who you are, and I had been ashamed for so long.

Can't Fight This Feeling

By the time I reached my teens, I had concluded that if I was with a good-looking white guy, I would be better accepted, more popular, less of an outsider. I wasn't dating, but my junior high and high school infatuations were inevitably focused on the athletic, smart, and confident boys—always white. Never mind that I was awkward in my older sister's pink handmade *Miami Vice*–inspired blazer, sporting a haircut given to me by my mother in the basement of our house and hiding behind large white-plastic-framed eyeglasses. A girl could dream.

Jack, a tall, blond-haired, blue-eyed boy with a sweet smile and a quiet disposition, was my first crush. I was in ninth grade. He played basketball. I spoke with him every chance I got in World History. Jack, his twin brother James, and their single mother lived in the trailer park across the field from the apartment complex where my family and I lived.

"Would you like to go to the school dance with me?" I asked him midyear, certain that he liked me.

He smiled at me shyly. "I'm sorry, I can't go."

I spent all of history class feeling rejected but refused to believe that he didn't like me. I knew he did. It didn't occur to me that perhaps he couldn't afford to go to the dance. I ended up attending the dance on my own and hanging with a few friends I saw there. I wore a pale-pink taffeta gown I'd found on clearance at the mall. I was brilliant in my shimmery dress.

At the end of the year, Jack and I traded yearbooks for signing. "Best wishes at South High. See you there!" I wrote in my best cursive.

He handed me back my yearbook with a smile, and we said our goodbyes. I hugged the book to my chest and boarded the bus, desperate to read what he had written. REO Speedwagon's "Can't Fight This Feeling" was playing on the driver's little radio as the bus exited the lot and trundled along the street. I cracked open my yearbook and scanned for Jack's note.

"I wish I had said yes when you asked me to the dance. I missed my chance to dance with you." I stared at his words the entire ride home, smiling and feeling hopeful. *He does like me! Maybe he'll ask me out next year.*

Those thoughts were dashed a few months later because, shortly after the start of tenth grade that fall, my family moved to the southeastern part of town. Jack and I ended up at different high schools.

I continued to have crushes, but I didn't date in high school. Life was too busy and complicated. I worked as a hostess and cashier at a restaurant popular for its pies and cakes. I was better off staying out of the house, earning my own money for books, clothes, and gas for my little Corolla. My interactions with my mother became increasingly strained as she continued to pressure me about college, my lukewarm devotion to the Catholic Church, and my dwindling contributions around the house. Any ideas I had about dating were quashed by my mother's constant nagging. The stress I felt living at home was crushing and only eased up when I was elsewhere.

When it came time to consider colleges, I could have applied to Wichita State University, fifteen minutes away on the north side of town, but I applied to schools that required me to move away from home. No way would I stay under my mother's roof. I ended up at the University of Kansas, a large public university two hours' drive away. It was a small but definitive step toward independence.

College became my new safe haven. I had spent high school fearful of my mother's wrath when it came to distractions (going out with friends) and misdeeds (not getting straight As), so life at university was sweet freedom. I went out with my new college friends and a few I had been acquainted with in high school. I didn't speak of my mother's abuse and my insecurities. My friends and I spent a great deal of time hanging out in our dorm rooms, inviting ourselves to house parties hosted by friends and strangers, and attending raucous basketball and football games. I was thrilled to slowly shed my staid life of school and work, school and work, finally allowing myself to relax and do as I please.

I spent a few blissful weeks of my freshman year dating a charming fellow from one of the fraternities on campus. Nick had the bluest eyes and was intrigued by Asian girls. I felt special dating him because he singled me out; he liked that I was Asian. With him, I didn't feel weird about myself; he made me feel normal. He liked my wildly permed hair and innocent grin. I felt beautiful.

I had heard there was a term for guys like Nick. He had Yellow Fever, a derisive reference describing white guys who dated Asian girls. If he had Yellow Fever, then what did I have? Was there a term for girls like me? Was my preference for athletic Kansas farm boys a type? Was White Fever a thing, too? Did I care what that said about me? Should I care?

When my family first moved to Kansas, I was just starting to view boys differently, to think of them as potential boyfriends. I was still open to the idea that boys, regardless of race or ethnicity, were attractive. In high school, however, my interest in them shifted and was eventually extinguished, obliterated by my desire to whitewash myself. I didn't feel I fit with them, so I rejected them. When Bao Chen, a Chinese American classmate, asked me to the prom at the end of our senior year, I told him, "I'd rather go by myself." I was trying to elevate myself. Going with another Asian student was not part of my program. I was a raging, self-hating bitch. Casualties were inevitable.

* * *

At the start of my sophomore year at KU, I spotted a tall, athletic neighbor of mine from the upstairs window in my apartment. I eventually made up an excuse to meet him—I went over to borrow some sugar one day. Kurt was dressed in tight-fitting bike shorts and was heading out when I rang the bell. He humored me and gave me some sugar, then excused himself to go for a ride with his friends.

From that contrived beginning, Kurt and I ended up going out to eat, seeing movies, and camping. He was from a Kansas City suburb; one of his parents was a law firm partner, and the other was a college instructor. He was an all-American boy wanting for nothing, gregarious in his laughter and always willing to try new things. In my nineteen-year-old mind, I had hit the dating jackpot. Never mind that he ended up dating another girl on the side, and I was willing to turn a blind eye.

More than a year into college, I hadn't shared much about my heritage with any of my friends. They knew I liked to read, didn't drink, and was a rule-follower, but I didn't describe the country I came from, the foods I ate growing up, the holidays we celebrated. The process of accepting my past and my ethnicity was a slow one, and with Kurt being my first boyfriend, I resisted revealing any Vietnamese aspects of my life to him.

"Tell me about your family," he asked early on.

"Well, I've got four brothers and two sisters."

"Wow, I have one brother. What was it like to grow up in such a big family?" I told him about our many fights and playing in the creek as kids in Florida.

"What's Vietnamese food like?" he asked.

I appreciated that he was curious, but I was still hesitant. "Well, there's this soup called *phở*. It's got rice noodles, sliced beef, onions, and cilantro, and the broth is made with lots of different spices."

"Sounds good. I'd like to try it." He drove us forty-five minutes into Kansas City to find a Vietnamese restaurant. He wanted to share the experience with me. I prayed in the car on the way there that the restaurant didn't serve the weird stuff that Vietnamese people eat, like tripe and other animal innards. I was nervous, and it struck me as unusual and unsettling that he would go out of his way to learn about my culture.

Kurt asked about me, my family, and my past. Yet I was still leery of his support and caring nature. I didn't want him to know too much about me, and I feared that telling him everything would make me vulnerable. I didn't want to be vulnerable to anyone. Life was easier if everyone assumed I was thick-skinned and had no deep, dark secrets. I didn't let myself believe he was being entirely sincere. I could not understand how a member of the majority would ever accept me as who I was, an immigrant, refugee, foreigner, but still American. I didn't see the correlation between his grandparents, who were from Germany and had immigrated to the United States, and my own family. In my mind, being in the United States for multiple generations was different, nothing like being newly arrived. How could anyone accept me when I could not even accept myself?

The college we attended was only thirty minutes from the suburb where he grew up. Some weekends, we met his parents and younger brother for lunch or dinner. It was Kurt's way of spending time with them, and it allowed them to get to know me. In addition to their regular jobs, his parents, Frank and Ida

Weber, ran a cattle farm on the outskirts of town. Their house
was filled with comfortable furniture, knickknacks, and family
portraits on the walls. It was a cozy, ideal home. It was the kind
of home I had wanted when I was growing up.

They paid for Kurt's schooling and provided him with an
allowance. He spent his money without ever worrying he would
run out. I felt guilty when he purchased a brand-new mountain
bike for me to join him on his rides and even worse when, on the
one outing I agreed to, I hit a rut in the trail and flew over the
bike, injuring myself and cutting the ride short in the process.
I ruined the ride for him and his friends who had come along.
Though he'd gotten me that bike out of generosity and kindness,
I was not a fan of mountain biking and saw the gift, which cost
the equivalent of three months' rent for my apartment, as a waste
of money. I blanched at the thought of riding after that incident.

When I met them, Kurt's parents asked me a lot of questions.

"Where is your family from?"

"What does your mother do?"

"What did your father do before he passed away?"

"What are your plans for the future?"

"How long have you lived in the States?"

"Do you speak Vietnamese?"

"How many siblings do you have?"

I answered as honestly as I could, but I kept my replies as
scant or vague as I could make them, afraid his parents would
judge me as being too far beneath their eldest son. I had been
asked those questions in the past, by strangers and by friends'
parents. I hated them because I never felt any of my answers
spoke well of me, of my family, of our past. I felt the judgment
in them and thought that the person asking was only seeking
ways to fit me into some category they had constructed. In my
answers, the interrogator sought to validate whatever they believed, and my responses helped determine how I should be
treated and addressed.

Frank kept his distance and didn't engage in much conversation with me, but I enjoyed getting to know Kurt's mother, despite my misgivings. Ida was a tall, sturdy woman, nurturing and soft-spoken. Very different from my own mother. She shared recipes with me and packed extra heaping plates of leftovers to take back with us. She once invited me out to their cattle farm, and I got to see their herd and operation. The Webers were proud of their accomplishments and the life they had built for themselves and their sons.

However hopeful and in love I may have been, it didn't take long to feel the sting of ethnic differences, of being viewed as inadequate. At Thanksgiving, Kurt invited me to join him at his parents' house for dinner. I didn't care to go home to my own family, so I readily accepted. It was my first invitation to a family gathering during a major holiday. I didn't know that to be deemed a gracious guest, I should bring a bouquet of flowers or a pie. I hadn't spent much time at friends' homes, so the rules of etiquette were foreign to me.

Wanting to make a good impression, I offered to help with the final preparations once we arrived. Ida directed me in whisking gravy in a saucepan over the stove. "I don't want you to get the wrong idea," she started to say. I hate when people start conversations that way; it's like saying, "No offense but . . ." or "We need to talk." Nothing good ever comes after such an opener. I held my breath as she continued, "But if you stay with Kurt, you will have a very hard time."

I looked at her, not sure what she was getting at.

"You're a lovely young lady, but mixed-race couples . . . they don't work. People don't understand . . . You'll be mistreated, and so will my son."

I didn't know what to say, so I remained silent.

"His father and I have high expectations for Kurt. If you love him, you should let him go." She patted me on the shoulder, as if to convey how sorry she was that the world was so unfair.

I found it utterly ironic that she would warn me against possible mistreatment when it seemed she herself would rather not support our relationship or champion it on our behalf. Though she didn't say it out loud, I felt she didn't have any expectations of me, high or low. It was as if she doubted I'd amount to anything. I came from nothing, and I would end up the same way I had started.

With the entire dinner still ahead of us, I could only nod as if I agreed. I kept my eyes cast down, trying not to cry and pretending to focus on making the best damn gravy ever.

It was a long, thankless meal. We sat down at the round table laden with aromatic and scrumptious dishes. We bowed our heads and said grace before eating. I pushed mashed potatoes and turkey around on my plate, taking small bites while my mind was a million miles away, turning Ida's words over and over until it was time to leave.

I didn't share with Kurt what his mother said that day. I was embarrassed by how she highlighted our racial and socioeconomic differences and feared that he would agree with her.

Despite what his mother said at Thanksgiving, I continued my relationship with Kurt. I wanted desperately to hang on to this dating jackpot. Some months later, my mother, who had up to that time avoided visiting me at college, decided to come up for the day. She hadn't moved me into my dorm room when I started as a freshman; that honor was left to my friend Maria's mother. I was happy to have my life without my mom in it. Now I was well into my sophomore year, and she might have heard some inkling of joy in my voice during our rare and brief calls. Mom must have suspected I was not entirely studious. "I'm coming up. I need to see you and meet your friends," she declared over the phone.

I hadn't breathed a word of having a boyfriend, knowing it would lead to no kind words on her part, so when she met Kurt, I lumped him in with a few of my girlfriends. "And this is Kurt, another friend of mine, and he happens to be my neighbor." I was never good at lying, and I know she caught on right away. But she pasted a smile on her face and treated us all to the Chinese buffet across town. We ate until we were near bursting, and I ignored furtive glances shot my way by my girlfriends, who surrounded Kurt to keep up the illusion that he was most certainly not my boyfriend. I warned him that she was critical of everything I did, and he was willing to play along if it meant I would not suffer her wrath later. He did his best not to be too friendly, but he still tried to get my mom to warm up to him, asking her questions and generally being nice. "So, Mrs. Pham, how was your drive up to Lawrence?"

That evening, before she left to drive back to Wichita, I got an earful from her.

"Keep away from that tall boy. I saw him looking at you. You guys don't fool me."

"I don't know what you're talking about, Mom," I said, trying to sound nonchalant about Kurt. "He's just my neighbor. You have nothing to worry about."

"He's white. And he's not Catholic, for God's sake!" She was clearly not letting this go. "You need to marry a good Vietnamese Catholic man. You need to keep the Vietnamese traditions alive. You need to have Vietnamese babies and teach them our language. That's how it should be."

I stayed quiet. It wasn't enough that Kurt's parents had "high expectations" for him; my mom had her own set of expectations for me. Expectations I had little intention of meeting; I simply did not care to date Vietnamese guys.

"Aren't there any smart Vietnamese boys around here for you to get to know?" she continued, then thought better of it. "But you're still young, and you have to finish college. Stay away from boys. You hear me? Stay away from boys."

Once she was gone, I went next door and told Kurt what she'd said.

"My mom knows we're dating."

"Yeah?"

"She told me to focus on school and that I shouldn't be with you."

"Why not?"

"You're not Vietnamese."

He laughed.

"Seriously. She wants me to marry a Vietnamese guy and have Vietnamese babies."

"Why does that matter?"

"It just does."

At Thanksgiving, I hadn't been able to bring myself to reveal to him what his own mother had said, yet here I was, confessing my own mother's biases. I appreciated that he didn't see any problems with us being a biracial couple, but I was caught between two mothers who wanted nothing but for their children to stick to their own kind. What was a girl to do?

Weekend Pursuits

About two months into dating Kurt, he received a letter from someone named Carrie Ann Jones. These were the days before email and mobile phones, before texting and Facebook. I remember her name well because she wrote it with a flourish in large cursive letters on the envelope.

"Who's Carrie Ann Jones?" I asked, trying to sound casual.

"Oh, she's just a friend of mine," Kurt replied, trying just as hard to be casual.

He tucked the letter away in his back pocket, clearly intending to read it out of my sight. He never mentioned what she wrote, but I watched as he dropped his reply into the mail on our way out a couple of days later.

A few weeks passed, and he received another letter. He again tucked it away and read it when I was not around. I hated that this Carrie girl was writing to my boyfriend. She had the audacity to write to someone who was spoken for. And I hated her even more for having so much confidence that it showed in her penmanship, but still, I kept quiet about my jealousy. I should have hated my boyfriend for writing her back.

Over winter break, Kurt informed me that he was going to

Kansas City for the weekend. At this point in our relationship, we spent nearly every free moment together, parting only for classes and other absolutely necessary tasks, so it came as a surprise that he was going somewhere and I was not invited.

"What are you doing in Kansas City?" I asked, again trying to sound casual. Casual was my middle name. I would not let jealousy ruin my relationship.

"Just going to see a friend," he said, again trying equally hard to be casual.

I had a hunch about who this friend was. "Would it happen to be Carrie?"

Caught, he admitted that he was going to see her. "But we're just friends. I'm just hanging out with her like I would hang out with my guy friends."

"And what are you guys going to be doing?"

"Just hanging out. Maybe we'll go out to eat or see a movie."

Damned if that didn't sound like a date. I was uncomfortable about the entire arrangement, but this was my first real relationship, so I attempted to go the not-possessive-girlfriend route.

"OK, well, have fun."

I ended up moping around my apartment that weekend, wondering how my boyfriend's date was going. I was pathetic. When he returned at the end of the weekend, I asked him if he had fun, and he said, "Yes, I did." And left it at that.

Several months into our relationship, we were finishing up the school year and preparing for summer break. I intended to stay in Lawrence to work my part-time job at a kitchen goods store downtown. I also planned to retake a chemistry course I had gotten a D in. I needed to get a higher grade, fearful I'd amount to nothing if the grades on my transcripts were horrible. I don't recall what Kurt's plans were, aside from biking, but he dropped a bombshell on me one afternoon.

"I love you, Hong," he started. "But I also have feelings for Carrie."

OK. Deep breath.

"I was thinking that I'd like to date her, too."

It seemed to me they had already been dating, but I had remained steadfast in my portrayal of the not-possessive, not-at-all-jealous girlfriend, so this was my passive attitude blowing up in my face. This was also his way of laying it all out for discussion.

"Hear me out," he said as I sat staring at him. I was not one for this kind of talk. "I believe that a person can have more than one soul mate. And it's quite possible that you and Carrie are both my soul mates. I want you both in my life."

"You're fucking crazy" was all I could say before I started crying. I was young, insecure, and thought I'd found "the one." I had grown up on fairy tales and happily ever after, so this announcement from my boyfriend was like a knife to my heart. I hadn't had much happiness to cling to and thought that love really would conquer all. I was devastated that he wanted me to share his affections.

We argued at length about his revelation, and in the end, we continued dating, and he may or may not have informed Carrie that I would not share. I had won that battle, or so I thought.

He went to Kansas City a few times that summer, likely to see her, but I chose not to inquire. On one of his excursions, I snooped around his bedroom. I had a key to his place and decided to find out for myself what she had been saying in her letters. He kept his correspondence in a box in his closet, and I sat on the floor, poring over the many pages she had sent.

It was a violation of privacy, but I felt entitled to read those letters and believed I was smart to educate myself. The contents of one particular letter stunned me. There were pages and pages of stupid stuff, but what caught me off guard was her brazen statement about masturbating to thoughts of him and reaching orgasm within minutes. My Catholic-girl mentality recoiled at such vulgar words. I was a prude and never spoke like that to him, sure I would burn in a hotter level of hell than I was already destined for. Here, in her letters, she was saying these things. How dare she be so bold? So unlike me?

I was furious. *Fuck Carrie Ann Jones.* If she was "just a friend," why on earth was she speaking of masturbating? But if I knew they weren't just friends, why was I willing to live with this arrangement? I was angry at them. But I was also angry at myself.

"How was your weekend with your friend Carrie?" I asked when he came back to Lawrence, spitting out her name at the end.

"Fine. We had fun, but I wasn't with her the whole weekend, you know."

"Sure you weren't."

"What's that supposed to mean?"

"It means I know what she's been writing to you! I read her letters."

"Those are my private letters. You have no right to go through my stuff!"

Around and around we went. He was upset that I had gone through his letters, while I was upset that he didn't understand why I was hurt. I hated how spineless I was, yet I wasn't willing to leave, and that made me hate myself even more.

*   *   *

As the child of an alcoholic, I was cautious about my consumption of beer, wine, hard liquor, and anything else that would impair my judgment. When I went out with friends, I was their designated driver. On the few occasions that I drank, I would fall asleep in the corner or beg to leave early. Drinking also made me act foolishly, made me feel brave, and that was a frightening prospect. I was reserved and level-headed. I didn't want my friends to see me behave otherwise.

I had never smoked marijuana or tried any other recreational drugs when I started college. Toward the end of our relationship, Kurt discovered the joys of smoking pot. He kept it from me at first, knowing I would disapprove. He started spending more time with his friends, and I returned to hanging out with my girlfriends.

Marijuana became a sore point for me when he drove while high one day, arriving at my door completely spaced out and loose as a jellyfish. I argued with him about his irresponsibility in driving across town in his state.

"You should have called me! I would have come to pick you up!"

I was livid, but he was too high to understand where I was coming from.

Kurt spent a great deal of time smoking and searching for himself as the semester progressed. He was a sophomore, and I was a year ahead. At this point, we had called it quits a few times, only to reconcile and resume our rocky relationship.

He eventually dropped out of school, sold his collection of music CDs, and gave away other possessions. His plans for the future got hazy. I revealed to him that I intended to apply to graduate school, which meant I would put my education before our relationship. Despite wanting to date Carrie Ann Jones while he was dating me, Kurt could not understand how I would so selfishly overlook his importance in my life, and I could not understand how he was so callow as to think we were always going to be together. We stopped dating. Our mutual friends expressed concern over his choices, but there was nothing I could do for him.

While I continued my studies, determined to finish college, Kurt packed up and moved to Durango, Colorado. His plan was to snowboard in the winter and bike in the summer. He would work odd jobs to earn money to live on. I imagined that his parents were not too keen on his decisions, and the thought occurred to me that Frank and Ida probably blamed me for his downfall.

As for my mother, the day I donned my cap and gown to receive my bachelor's degree, she gave me her usual one-shouldered hug and said, "Now it's time to find a husband and start a family." Apparently, she didn't think courtship was part of that equation. I had a lot more of life and living to do, and I clearly needed to take her view on things with a grain of salt. I only served to continue disappointing her because I didn't find a husband for another twelve years after graduating.

*　*　*

Though we had been broken up for nearly two years when I graduated from the University of Kansas, I didn't feel Kurt and I were done. We needed closure. I heard from mutual friends that he had gotten Durango out of his system and was thinking of moving to the Pacific Northwest. I had completed my senior thesis over the summer and decided I would move to Washington State. He was staying with his parents again in Kansas City, so I dropped by with a letter before I left for Seattle. I could say the idea of him planning to move to Olympia had nothing to do with my decision to move to Seattle, but that's a lie. A very tiny part of me thought maybe we could have a do-over.

In my letter, I expressed that I was sorry for all the bumps in our relationship, and I wished him well. I gave him my contact information and invited him to visit me in Seattle if he got lonely. A few months later, we were in my car in a parking lot at Alki Beach, facing the nighttime skyline of downtown Seattle. We talked about our past and our futures. Futures, as in separate paths. We had grown up a little in our time apart, and it was comfortable to be together again in a new place, even if we were no longer dating. That moment, in the quiet of my brand-new maroon Nissan Sentra, with the windows fogging up from the warm interior and cool exterior, we began to mend from the tumultuous time we had spent together in college.

We didn't rekindle our relationship, but we spent time together like a couple would. Our nonrelationship was far better than our actual dating relationship had ever been. We hiked the trails of Mount Rainier several times. We drove down to Oregon and camped on the misty slopes of Mount Hood. During our hikes and drives, we talked more openly about ourselves and our lives.

"Are you still applying to graduate school?" he asked me as we sat on a riverbank one evening.

"Nah, not yet. I didn't score very well on the GRE [Graduate Record Examination], and I need to get some work experience. Besides, I have school loans to pay off."

"Mmm," he replied.

"What about you?" I asked.

"I'll work for a bit. I don't know what I want to do with my life."

We sat quietly, listening to the water trickling over the rocks and pebbles in the creek.

"I'm sorry about the way I treated you. With Carrie, I mean. It was selfish of me to expect you to be OK with me dating you both."

"Yeah, that sucked."

It was strange to hear him say he was sorry, but I was glad to know that he finally understood my pain.

Spring Break with a Debutante

College gave me the chance to form stronger friendships than I'd had in high school, when I had been too busy trying to escape Wichita to commit to the deep bonds that I desperately wanted with my friends. Living in the dormitories my first year at the University of Kansas gave me the opportunity to meet girls who would become lifelong friends. Though a few hailed from the Kansas City area, many came from the same high school I had graduated from. These girls were my tribe. We studied, ate, and went out together.

Except for Iris and Ivy, sisters whose family was from the Philippines, I didn't make friends with any of the Asian girls at KU, though I knew some of them and saw them on campus. Iris and her roommate shared a dorm room that was a few doors down the hall from Hillary's and mine. Petite, soft-spoken, and gorgeous, with mesmerizing eyelashes, Iris was likable and kind to everyone. She didn't have an ounce of awkwardness to her or any of the refugee baggage that I carried around with me. I had spent years trying to be white, but when I met Iris, I decided that if I had to be Asian, I'd be her. I could pretend that I was clever, sweet, and congenial, just like Iris.

In the spring of my freshman year, my friend Margo and I decided to spend our weeklong break in Florida. There was an organized bus trip that would take us to and from Panama City Beach. This chance to see the beach of my childhood days again thrilled me.

Eager to hit the sand and surf in style, I went to Target and bought a new two-piece bathing suit. In black and hot pink, the top's boxy cut with a giant vertical plastic clip in the middle made my barely-there chest disappear altogether. The bottom was high-waisted and swallowed up my entire abdomen. It made me feel full of newfound sexiness. In truth, it was as sexy as a train wreck.

Margo was a debutante from a Chicago suburb. Her hair was a glossy golden wheat that sparkled, even in dimly lit rooms. When she smiled, her green-specked hazel eyes twinkled like stars, and her plump-lipped smile revealed perfectly straight white teeth. We both had moles, but hers was a dainty beauty mark on her cheek, whereas mine was a sizable lump that situated itself in the crease of my smile line below my right cheek. We were the same age, but Margo was all woman with her curves, whereas I looked like I had missed out on puberty altogether.

Excited for our trip, I modeled my new bikini for Margo.

"That's some bathing suit," she said after a beat. "Good for you." She really was the nicest friend.

I don't recall much of the bus ride down. We slept in between talking about her boyfriend, a tall and handsome football player, Chad, her high school sweetheart. She told me he and his friends had their own plans for the week. It wasn't until we arrived at our hotel in Panama City Beach that I discovered they had driven down behind our bus and Chad's plans included watching over Margo.

I thought he was being a good boyfriend to care enough to drive down, but what did I know? I didn't realize it was more out of jealousy than protectiveness. At that time, I'd only ever kissed one guy, a nice, sloppy kiss that ended an awkward night of not dancing at my junior homecoming. I dove headlong into college having never had a steady boyfriend.

The morning after we arrived, we quickly donned our respective bikinis, grabbed our towels, and ran down to the crowded beach to sunbathe. Margo lounged in her turquoise two-piece with its ruffles and bows, grinning at the sun. I planted my pale body on my own towel, skin prickling from nerves at showing so much skin. A group of six University of Kentucky boys rough-housed nearby with their game of Frisbee. They joked, laughed, and threw smiles in our direction. After a time, one of them approached me.

"Hi, I'm Auggie." Auggie was the shortest of the bunch, had a crooked nose and stubby toes. I blushed and wondered why he had come to speak to me. He smiled and ran his fingers through his messy blond hair. Then came the inquiry that would repeat itself many times over on this trip, uttered by countless besotted fellows with their beefy arms and tousled locks. "What's your friend's name?" he asked as he lifted his gaze to Margo and her tanned goddess body.

I can look back on the entire trip and laugh now, but as I sat on my beach towel with my toes in the sand, this one question mortified me. I felt all the lesser for being the ugly duckling next to the sweetest beach bunny from Chicago's high society.

Margo was destined for designer labels while I, not able to afford authentic collegiate apparel from the university bookstore, cut out felt letters to sew onto plain sweatshirts I had gotten at a discount store. Though she never treated me as a poor friend, I still felt the disparity in our socioeconomic standings. I needed to stop fooling myself and accept that I was no competition for gorgeous Margo and her country-club affluence.

It would be many more years before I'd figure out that I didn't need her flawless looks or wealth to charm anyone. I could learn practical life skills, read books, help those in need, and travel to far-flung places to become more attractive in my own way.

*　*　*

I struck up a friendship with a couple of guys in one of my classes in the winter of my senior year at the University of Kansas. Dave was a lean blond from the suburbs of Chicago. Jeff was a stocky, chestnut-haired fellow from Kansas City. I wasn't dating anyone, so it was fun to have two guys to hang out with who I felt treated me like a princess. I helped Dave and Jeff with class assignments, and they taught me how to Rollerblade. I got proficient enough on my skates to play inline hockey with them.

When I started sending out résumés for jobs, they took me to shop for an interview suit.

"Get this one," Jeff said when I'd walked out of the dressing room in a slimming black suit. "It looks really good on you."

"Yeah, you look great," Dave concurred.

It cost me around $200, eating up more than half of my monthly rent on the apartment I shared with Hillary, but with such compliments, how could I not buy the suit? I was anxious about finding a job, and I desperately needed help in the style department. I have no idea why I didn't recruit one of my girl-friends to help me shop, but no doubt, flattery from the two guys went a long way in easing my distress about my interviews. I had become fast friends with them, and I liked that they were willing to assist me in finding an outfit. We went out for drinks afterward.

"What would you like to have?" Dave asked me when we sat down at the restaurant.

"I don't know," I said. The truth was, I hardly drank. I was usually the designated driver when I went out with my girlfriends. Someone had to remain level-headed and get every-one home safe.

"Let's get you a whisky sour," Dave said.

I wanted the guys to think I was a big girl, brave enough to drink. I acquiesced, but a voice in the back of my mind rebelled, reminding me of my lifelong fear that I would become an alcoholic like my father was. The one drink was enough to get me tipsy, but I sobered up on the ride back to Lawrence. That might have been my first drink without my girlfriends around to shelter me from the harm I was sure I would suffer from alcohol. But nothing horrible happened, and life went on. I had proved I was a big girl after all.

One afternoon, Dave, Jeff, and I came out of class in the center of campus and made our way across the lawn where tables and booths were set up for Lunar New Year. I had not been involved in planning the celebration, but I was aware that it was taking place. I had just started working on my senior thesis for my degree in sociology, and the students I had approached for interviews had told me about it and invited me to join them. As I'd done every year prior, I opted out of attending. I felt the Asian students were a clique of their own, and I never seemed to fit in with them, so I made excuses.

Students were looking at red envelopes and reading display boards about the celebration. There was a line for Chinese and other Asian foods being served. Large speakers had been placed in one corner, and an unfamiliar song played at high volume. The crowd was thick, and we had to navigate around clumps of students to get through.

"What the fuck is all this?" Dave exclaimed as he took in our surroundings.

"Um . . . it looks like they're set up for Chinese New Year," I said hesitantly.

"Well, they've taken over the whole fucking place," he concluded.

I wasn't sure why he took offense to the event, and I didn't understand his reaction. I grew up celebrating Tết, Vietnamese Lunar New Year. My ego stung from the attack on a tradition I had once cherished. I had tucked away that aspect of my heritage, not sure I wanted to reveal myself for the ethnic minority that I was. I knew in my heart that they could see I was Asian, but I had long ago convinced myself I was as white and American as they were. I could have suggested we stop to look around, to share the holiday with them, but instead, I chose to keep silent.

I parted ways with Dave and Jeff that afternoon and went home. That was the last time we walked together as friends.

The next day, we had planned to play inline hockey on the newly paved lot at the recently built auditorium across campus. When they showed up at my apartment and rang my doorbell, I refused to answer.

"Come on, Hong. Open the door."

It was childish of me, but in that moment, I didn't know how to express my disappointment at what Dave had said the day before.

"Open up! We know you're home!"

I had never learned to communicate openly, and so I thought it was better to hide behind the door and hold my breath until they gave up and left.

After that, I avoided them on campus, which wasn't easy when I saw them in class. They must have worked out a plan to figure out my beef, because Jeff approached me one day and asked why I was no longer speaking to him and Dave.

"I've been busy," I told him.

"Did we do something?" Jeff asked. "Why aren't you hanging out with us? What happened?"

"I don't think we should be friends anymore." I stopped myself from adding, "Dave is a jerk, and there's nothing wrong with people celebrating Lunar New Year."

Jeff was soft-spoken, so I didn't expect him to put up a fight. In the end, the guys gave up on me and our friendship. I wished that I could have spoken up for myself and expressed my feelings, but that would have required me to admit to them that I was Vietnamese. In only a few more weeks, I would sit down to interview my thesis subjects, and my eyes would be opened to the truth behind my ethnic background, the struggles of Southeast Asians who were willing to risk dying, escaping communism to live a better life. I would learn the strength of my people and their determination to strive for the American dream while never forgetting where they came from. But until then, I was a chicken, hiding from the guys, from my past, and from myself.

Office Hours

Even as a kid, I knew the drill about career choices. I needed to be a doctor, a lawyer, or an engineer when I grew up. My mother was adamant that I would succeed professionally while simultaneously causing me to feel like I would amount to nothing. Witnessing her struggles as a single parent to seven kids, I vowed I would not end up like her. I would study hard, become a successful professional, and live comfortably. Also, I would avoid having seven kids.

It was my mother's fervent hope that one of us kids would become a doctor, so despite defying her wishes that I stay home for college, I at least appeased her by choosing a premed study program. I suffered through math and science courses, scoring low on tests and wishing for the end of each semester to come sooner. I despaired of ever enjoying my classes and wondered, seriously and often, why I was trying so hard to go the premed route. After all, I disliked the disinfectant smell of hospitals, hated the sight of blood and open wounds, and was miserable at the thought of working in the medical field.

I spent the summer after my sophomore year retaking a chemistry class. During office hours one day, I approached my chemistry professor for guidance.

"So, what's the issue?" she asked abruptly before my bottom even hit the chair.

"Well, I've been struggling in Chemistry, and I retook your class this summer to bump up my D to a C. I still can't make heads or tails of your lectures," I confessed.

"And what do you want me to do about it?"

"Umm, well, I'm premed, you see, so I need help to understand this stuff. My mom really wants me to be a doctor one day."

She was a tenured professor who had no doubt heard the same pathetic whining from other students. Perhaps that day, she was fed up with our immaturity and lack of direction, because her response was direct and not what I wanted to hear: "Maybe you're just not cut out to be a doctor. Change majors. Move on." And with that, she dismissed me from her office.

While her advice was exactly what I needed, it was not delivered in an empathetic way, and I was crushed. In my young, impressionable mind, her words translated to, "You're wasting my time. Get out." I felt dejected and stupid. I had convinced myself that as an Asian, I had to be, was born to be, good at math and science. My teachers had told me I was. The stereotypes about Asian prowess in those subjects, from books and television shows, had seeped into not just their psyches but also my own. But that stereotype was far from true. I had only ever enjoyed geometry in high school, and physics was fun just because I had a dynamic and dedicated teacher.

After two years of poor grades in college, I lost my merit scholarship and was left without critical funds to pay for school. Starting my third year, I worried about how I would earn my degree, and because I would need to take out more loans than I originally intended, I worried about how much debt I would be in just to do it. Loans would cover my tuition and books, but it was all useless if I couldn't pay rent.

Then I met Norman Yetman.

One of my classes at the start of junior year was Social Problems and American Values. It was an elective that fulfilled a liberal arts requirement. Professor Yetman exuded understanding and patience. The coursework fascinated me; we were looking at America through a sociological lens, and I ate up the subject matter. Poverty, gender, crime, race relations: all the ugly bits of American society were dissected. Having felt so lost as an Asian growing up among white people, I longed to figure out how I would fit in better, more comfortably. I loved that the subject matter was frank, that the class was willing to look deeply into problems and seek out reasons for them, and that awareness of these issues was the first step toward making society a better place.

Professor Yetman struck me as someone I could trust and look up to for guidance, so I decided to pay him a visit during office hours.

"Come in. Sit down." He gestured to a chair in front of his desk. I took the seat, and we looked at each other over his desk. I fidgeted with my backpack before setting it down by my feet. I hadn't thought through what to say. I only knew I needed advice.

Sensing my unease, he leaned forward and asked, "How can I help you today?"

"Well, sir, I hate science, and I don't want to be premed anymore."

"OK," he responded.

"And I'm really liking your class, so I wanted to ask you about maybe switching majors."

"What do you like about my class?" he asked, and from there, we launched into a discussion about sociology and American studies, both areas he did research in, wrote about, and taught.

I didn't know it when I walked in, but meeting with Norm, as I would come to call him after I graduated, would change my life. He gave me guidance on coursework and changing my major, and even more important to me at that time, he referred me to someone who might have a job for me after I explained my financial predicament.

Days after talking to Norm, I met his wife, Anne, and her business partner, Gunda Hiebert. Together, they owned a kitchen goods store in downtown Lawrence called the Bay Leaf. They sold all manner of kitchen gadgets, cookware, dishes, and utensils, along with coffee and tea. It was the mom-and-mom version of Sur la Table, except Sur la Table will never be as dear to me as the Bay Leaf. I started work a week or two later. It was good to be gainfully employed and back on track.

About a month into my job at the Bay Leaf, I plucked up some courage. "Anne and Gunda, I wonder if I could get a raise?"

"Oh, really? And why should we give you a raise?" They looked at each other, communicating something unspoken, then looked at me.

"I am a hard worker. I get a lot done. I come on time. I'm good at ringing up customers because I count back change accurately. And I do everything you ask of me." I left out the part about how I really needed more money so I could pay my rent and bills.

They were kind enough to agree to a marginal increase in my hourly pay, though I doubt I had offered enough evidence to warrant the raise.

Soon after that, during one of my shifts, Anne pointed across the counter to the opposite wall. "Hong, see the lady by the gadgets? Go ask her if you can help her find anything. And introduce her to the scraper. Tell her it's a gadget she shouldn't live without."

"Hong, while you're bagging and weighing out the coffee beans, suggest a second flavor," Gunda advised during a lull in the shop another afternoon. "Hazelnut is a hit, but chocolate macadamia is wonderful, too." In this way, Anne and Gunda helped me refine my customer service and retail skills. Not only that, but they were also models of how women ought to be. They were strong and hardworking, just like my mother, but they were also generous and compassionate. I was proud to say I worked at the Bay Leaf because it was a favorite in the community and very popular.

Gunda had a son away at college whom I saw once, maybe twice. The Yetmans had two children not much older than me, a son and a daughter. I met Doug and Jill when they were home from out-of-state college. In them, I saw two very fortunate kids who were loved, guided, and encouraged by caring parents. They were knowledgeable and confident, and I envied them.

Doug helped out during Christmas season, when the store was especially busy with holiday shoppers. One day we were in the back by the teas and coffees, tidying up and stocking the shelves. Doug was charismatic and fun to work with, and I found myself really enjoying his company. A song came on over the store's sound system.

"Oh, I love this song!" he said as he started singing along.

It was Ella Fitzgerald's "The Lady Is a Tramp," but at the time, I didn't know the song. Doug sang along with gusto while I was deep in thought. I'd never heard of mulligan stew, but I had certainly wished for turkey instead of *phở* and spring rolls during the holidays. I'd never been to Maine or Albuquerque. I didn't have a clue who "Bozart" was and why his or her ball was all the rage. I remembered learning about Noël Coward in high school drama class, though I had no idea what or where hobohemian was.

"Come on—sing along with me!" he said in between belting out the lyrics.

"I don't know this song," I told him. "Never heard it before, in fact."

"Seriously?" Doug responded.

I had never listened to jazz, my music exposure having been whatever rock songs were playing on the radio, except for the few years that included classical songs I learned when Mom had paid for my younger sister, Hạnh, and me to study piano. I was embarrassed that I wasn't familiar with jazz music and mortified that I had to admit my ignorance.

Though I had despaired of relationships, I thought Doug was cute, and in that moment, lost in the embarrassment of my lack of culture, I felt how far he was out of my league. I was the child of poor country folks who hailed from a small village in Việt Nam. My parents had not studied beyond grade school. My father, the fisherman, was long dead, and my mother cleaned homes for a living. How would I ever be good enough for the son of a respected university professor and an entrepreneur? He was a really nice guy but essentially another Kurt Weber, and I was still just poor little me. I was kidding myself if I thought we had anything in common.

Adding to my mixed emotions was the fact that I saw Anne and Norm as my surrogate parents. They offered advice about postcollege prospects, coursework, and friends. They didn't criticize; they didn't hurt me. They were the parents I had always wanted. To them, I was an adopted daughter, brought into the fold. Who was I to also wish that their son might consider asking me out on a date?

Examining Cultural Identity

When we first met in his office, Professor Yetman asked questions about my family, my past, and my goals.

"Your last name is Nguyen, so you're from Vietnam?"

"Yes, I am."

"When did you come to the US?"

"In 1975, at the end of the Vietnam War." I held my breath, praying he wouldn't ask for details, because I had none to offer.

"Did your entire family leave Vietnam? Do you still have family there?"

Relief. I could answer that. "My mom's dad was sick, so he stayed back, and my mom's younger sister stayed to take care of him."

"Mmm. What do your parents do for a living?"

"My dad died when I was eight. My mom runs a housekeeping business." No need to mention my dad was an abusive drunk or that Mom was the one doing the cleaning. All through high school, I had hated that my mom worked as a housekeeper for several families in the better part of town, where many of my classmates lived. I helped her clean when she was able to guilt me into it. I would dust slowly while admiring the way white families lived in homes with bedroom sets that matched. I imagined my own bedroom with matching furniture: a headboard, a pair of side tables, and chests of drawers. I wanted to have grown up in those homes with the impeccably manicured lawns and three-car garages, not in my family's squat, brown-brick house with rust-colored window shutters and a single-car garage. Here I was, in my professor's office, doing a pathetic job of pretending I was better than the daughter of a drunk and a housekeeper.

"Where is your mom now?"

"In Wichita."

"Do you have any siblings?"

"Yes, I have four brothers and two sisters." It never stopped sounding like too many kids.

"How old were you when your family left Vietnam?" *Oh God, we're back to that.*

"I was two or three years old."

"What does that mean?"

"Well, on paper, I was born in 1973, but I found out at the end of high school that I was born in 1972."

I went on to explain how my parents fled Việt Nam without official papers like birth certificates, so they likely made educated guesses when asked by the officials who processed our immigration applications.

I liked Professor Yetman a lot, so I spoke about my career aspirations and the classes I wanted to take. I never shared that my mom was physically abusive because it was a deeply personal subject, and I had convinced myself years before that corporal punishment wasn't really abuse. Though I hadn't yet matured enough to forgive her, I had told myself that my mother's beatings were simply her way of parenting.

Even as years passed and we grew close, I still withheld truths from Norm, afraid he would look at me differently. I wanted to be as much of a blank slate to him as I could be, not realizing that he likely knew my story without me having to say anything; he was, after all, a well-read educator and researcher in the fields of sociology and race relations. But believing that I was duping him allowed me the power to rise above the hurt I felt and the confusion I suffered from the experiences I had growing up. I was hoping I would feel normal if he treated me just like any of his other students.

Shortly after my first meeting with Norm, I switched majors and declared I would graduate with a bachelor of arts in sociology. I could no longer deny that medical school was a lost cause for me. In my final year, with a fresh slew of As and Bs on my transcript from taking courses I cared about and enjoyed, Norm encouraged me to work on a senior thesis project so that I could graduate with departmental honors. Graduating with honors in sociology would boost my chances of getting into a graduate school program. I thought I would be like Norm and become a sociologist, maybe even teach at a university one day.

"You've never talked about how your family came to America," Norm commented one day in a meeting with me to discuss possible thesis topics.

"Well," I said, "that's because I don't know much about our journey to America. We never talk about it in my family."

"Are you OK with that? Not talking about it?"

"It's probably important for my siblings and me to know details, but I hardly have enough Vietnamese words in my vocabulary to ask my mom about it, and her English is pretty limited."

"I see," he said. Then he added, "Do you have friends who immigrated to the US like you did? Do you ever talk to them about their experiences?" He wrongly assumed I had friends from Southeast Asia.

"Professor Yetman, I don't ever talk to my friends about such things. They would not be able to relate to any of it." It was then that he came to understand that I didn't have friends from Việt Nam or any of Việt Nam's neighboring countries.

"Would you like to know what your peers, other students

from Southeast Asia, think? How they feel? Would you like to
hear about their journeys?"

"You think that's a good thesis topic?"

"Absolutely," he said.

"Can I ask them how they identify themselves? Like, do they
feel they're Asian, or do they feel they're American?"

"Why not?"

In his wisdom and through our various conversations, Norm
discerned that I had long struggled to figure out who I was and
where I fit into the larger picture. I no longer felt like the little
girl who was called "chink" by kids pulling up the outer edges
of their eyes to make them slanted, but there was a void where I
should have felt some semblance of identity and self. I had done
such a good job of burying those incidents as a kid that I found
myself, in college, suddenly faced with examining this void and
wondering how it had grown so big. Maybe I hadn't actually
gotten past being called names and made fun of.

"I can't believe I can write a paper about cultural identity,"
I mused.

"Hong, cultural identity is a very important and interesting
subject."

When I made my choice in thesis topic, we both knew it
would give me some clarity, if not a better frame of reference, to
help me define my own cultural foundations.

My thesis sought answers to a complicated question: How
do Southeast Asian students at the University of Kansas identify
culturally?

I wanted to know whether they saw themselves as Americans
first or Asians first. And I wanted to know why. At the core of
it, I wanted to know if they were comfortable in their own skins.
These were my peers, students I had seen around campus. Some
I knew personally but did not associate with, having more often
than not distanced myself out of my own inner turmoil, not

because they weren't likable. I didn't hang out with them because I hadn't bothered to put in the effort to be friends, afraid they would discover I wasn't Asian enough.

When I approached to ask them to meet with me, more students than I anticipated were willing and open to the idea of speaking about race, culture, and identity. With my study subjects lined up, I started interviewing them one on one. We sat on the steps of the buildings on campus, and they shared their stories with me.

Vithu, a Cambodian guy I had known since junior high school when I first moved to the Midwest, was a fellow university student who agreed to tell me about his past. I did not realize until I sat down with him for my thesis project that I hardly knew him. I had spoken to him briefly when we ran into each other on campus, but we were not friends.

"I was ten when my family moved from Cambodia to Vietnam," he started. "My parents wanted to escape what was happening under the Khmer Rouge."

I made quick notes in my book.

"My parents heard about other families whose children had managed to reach the US and other Western countries, so they sent me and my sister, Rangsei, to the coast. Rangsei and I trekked like vagabonds until we reached the coast. In the dead of night, with the money our parents had saved up and given us, my sister and I paid a fee and slipped into a fishing boat, bound for the open sea."

"Where did the boat take you?"

"Nowhere, really. The goal was to get out far enough to be found by Good Samaritans who might be willing to help us seek refuge in a neighboring country. Though we had managed to get out of Cambodia, we still had the Vietnamese government to worry about. Any attempted escape had to happen in darkness. We were afraid we'd be caught and subjected to reeducation—or worse, death." This was in the mid-1980s, when the Vietnamese government was well into its practice of cracking down on dissent, locking up and torturing those who tried to escape.

"What happened on the boat?" I asked.

"The fishing boat was crowded with men, women, and children. We couldn't move around freely, and people would soil themselves as they sat crammed together in the rickety wooden vessel. It smelled so bad. Pee, poop, body odor. When the boat ran out of fuel, we drifted out at sea for days without food and very little water. Then the weak started to fade away, and a few of them died."

I remained quiet, not sure whether I should ask anything or let him continue.

"Then things got worse. Pirates came upon our boat and proceeded to strip us of what little we had—money and trinkets that had been tucked into secret compartments sewn into our clothes. The pirates knew about this clever concealment of valuables, having pillaged other boats, and they ripped our clothes from our bodies in their quest to find loot.

"We were hungry and delirious. We couldn't fight them," Vithu recalled, his focus shifting from me to the distance. I held my breath as he paused. I could see him watching the scene unfold, as if it were a movie. His face fell, and his eyes filled with tears.

"They raped Rangsei," Vithu said quietly to me, choking on his words. "I couldn't do anything to stop them. To help her."

We sat in silence as he relived his nightmare. I was at a loss for words, wholly unprepared to delve into the trauma of his escape. My greatest grief had been when my father died, but I was in the third grade, too young to have his death devastate me like this.

As for my own family's immigrant story, I called my older sister when I first started working on my thesis.

"Hey, can you tell me how our family got out of Việt Nam? How we ended up in America?"

"Why do you want to know?" she asked.

"For a school project. I'm writing a paper."

"Our family was picked up by a US Navy carrier. We ended up in Guam at a refugee camp before we were sent to Fort Chaffee, Arkansas. We got a lot of help from the Catholic Church." Her summation was detached and perfunctory. Weren't there any interesting anecdotes or traumatizing events? Compared to Vithu's journey, ours was a breeze.

Now, as I sat with him, I felt dreadfully stupid and ashamed of myself for thinking so little of the many newly arrived refugee students I met when I first started junior high school. He had been one of them. I learned to conjugate English verbs and diagram sentences with them, ate lunch with them, and saw them daily for an entire school year, yet I knew nothing of their struggles to escape terrible circumstances and find a better life. Even when I sat with them as their peer counselor, their stories did not sink into my young mind. Instead of getting to know them, I saw them as lesser than me because they had just arrived in the country, and I wanted to distance myself from them. Of the hundreds of refugee students who attended my junior high school, I only made friends with a handful, but we didn't talk about their journeys to America. I hadn't cared to ask.

Bé was a quick learner. Thúy-Lan liked fashion. Sơn was focused on becoming a doctor one day. Maybe it was because I didn't ask, but it might have also been that they didn't want to talk about their pasts, their journeys to the United States. Maybe they didn't want to relive it, like Vithu was doing as we sat on the gray concrete steps behind the building where I had taken Western Civilization.

"How do you identify yourself culturally?" I asked him.

Vithu sat quietly, thinking, before he said to me, "I'm Cambodian. I'll always be Cambodian. But I went through a lot to be American, so I guess I see myself as both."

"You don't see yourself as more of one than the other?" I asked.

"Neither is better than the other," he told me, "but my goal is to take the best of both and make it work. There's no sense in dwelling on my past, but it's a part of me. It shapes me and how I see my future."

He stopped speaking. I jotted notes in my book while the birds chirped and the breeze rustled the leaves in the trees. His gaze went across the lawn to the side of the building as he continued, "I don't want the struggles of my escape to overshadow what I can achieve. It would be a waste if I don't do something with my life, you know?"

I had spent so much of my life wishing I was white, trying to erase my Asian self. For years, I struggled with how I saw myself and how I wanted others to see me. Here was Vithu, already seeing that it didn't matter how much of either he should be. Instead, he wanted to channel his energy into being the best version of himself. I really needed to take a page from his book and start doing the same.

I completed the interviews during the last semester of my senior year, working them in between classes. My interview subjects sometimes told stories like Vithu's, heavy with tragedy and sadness. Other interviewees gave simple answers, neither going into detail nor offering much emotion, and I hardly scratched the surface with a few of them. I got the sense that perhaps the more reluctant subjects were like me—they didn't want to divulge secrets and internal struggles.

I found that my questions allowed the students to reflect on and consider their culture and identity in a way that some of them had not done before. I learned that they all shared some aspects of my own childhood, such as my troubles with my mother and even my struggle to fit the model-minority stereotype. Asians were expected to be smart, good at math and science. We had to be well behaved and obedient, not just within our families but also in school and in public. We were expected to be law-abiding citizens who would achieve success and contribute to our communities and society. It was a lot of pressure on our collective shoulders.

I saw aspects of myself in them, and they in me. Their comments and reflections mirrored many of the thoughts and experiences I had growing up:

"The kids in grade school used to tease me about the shape of my eyes."

"I hated giving book reports in middle school because I didn't want my classmates to focus on me, to see my hand-me-down clothes or worn-out shoes."

"Yeah, a few kids in my high school used to call me 'gook' and 'chink,' so I got into fights, which meant I got in trouble."

My Asian peers came together as a result of those experiences and built strength in numbers. But while they gravitated toward one another, I was busy retreating and hiding my ethnicity and culture, naively pretending I was anything but Asian so that I could blend in with the dominant culture.

As I worked on my thesis, I agonized over how to distill their words and views without diluting what they expressed. I was afraid my project would do them a disservice, that I wasn't cut out to say all the things they said. I was one of them but not at all. They were too busy striving to achieve their goals and dreams to be bogged down by the idea that race and ethnicity were limitations. Their successes, by way of degrees and careers, would speak for them. Vithu had said as much about himself. I realized during that project that I had been horribly wrong in how I treated my fellow Asian Americans. I had failed to embrace and appreciate the strength and pride that could be found in owning your identity, whether by birth or by circumstance.

*69

Late on a Friday night, shortly before the end of my senior year at KU, I received a call on the apartment's landline. My roommate Hillary was away for the weekend, having gone back to Olathe to see her family and her boyfriend. I didn't have plans with any other friends and had stayed home to read and catch up on school assignments.

"Hello?"

"Hellooo?" the male caller slurred.

"Yes, hello." I wasn't sure what else to say.

"Who's thisss?" the male caller asked.

"Who's this?" I asked in return.

"No one," he said. Then added, "What's your name?"

"Hong," I said reflexively, then realized immediately that I was an idiot for telling this stranger my name. Had I not watched enough movies to know you never give your name to a stranger? I heard rustling sounds and then a muffled, "Her name is Hong!" followed by laughter. The caller had covered the receiver to talk to some people on his side. He and his friends sounded drunk.

"What kind of name is that?" He was back.

"It's Vietnamese."

Rustling sounds again. Then, "She says it's Vietnamese."

"Ooh, ooh, ask her if she eats dogs!" I could hear another male voice call out.

"Do you eat dog?" my caller asked into the phone. Laughter on the other end.

"Seriously? What kind of question is that?" I demanded. *What the hell was wrong with these guys?*

"Well, do you?" he pressed on.

"No, I don't, you asshole." Then, in a fit of anger, I added, "Screw you!"

"Screw you!" he retorted. *Ugh. What on earth was happening?*

"Listen, I don't know who you are, but you're being racist, and I'll report you if you don't leave me alone."

"I'm just kidding, bitch."

Click. He had hung up on me. I slammed down the receiver and stared at the phone, fuming over what had just transpired. What a bunch of racist assholes. Stereotyping me and asking me if I ate dogs. I was not going to let them get away with this. I picked up the receiver and dialed *69. Last-call return was a brilliant feature available on landlines in those days before caller ID, and I fully intended to cuss out these drunk guys for their racist prank call.

I breathed hard as I waited for them to pick up. After the fourth unanswered ring, I hung up. Then, deciding I simply could not let this go, I picked up the phone again and dialed *69 a second time. On the third ring, someone answered.

"Hello?" A different male voice. Not nearly as intoxicated, it seemed.

"You hung up on me." I didn't care that he wasn't the jerk who had called.

"Dude, she called back." I heard what sounded like the phone being passed to someone else.

"How'd you get this number?" I recognized my prank caller's voice as he got back on the line.

"I dialed *69, idiot," I told him.

At this point, my goal was to get him and his friends to talk enough so that I could gather from their conversation who they were and where they were calling from. I could hear him covering the phone as he asked his friends what to say. They quickly debated, and then he was back on. I thought maybe they were feeling contrite about harassing me.

"Hey, can you tell me what this means?" he asked.

"What *what* means?"

"Ching chong chink chink chong chong." Guffaws on the other end of the line.

"What the hell was that? Are you trying to speak Vietnamese?"

"Look, bitch, you're the one who called me back. If you can't take a joke, why the hell did you *69 me?"

"You think that saying shit like 'ching chong' to me is funny? That's not funny. It's racist!"

"Well, I think it's funny, and so do my frat brothers." *Bingo.* I heard him suck in a breath when he realized his slipup. His fraternity brothers also caught his mistake.

"Where are you guys at? What fraternity are you in?" I was eager to hunt them down.

"Like I'm gonna tell you," he said and hung up again.

I called him back, but despite answering, he refused to speak further. In his silence, I told him I was going to find them and get them in trouble for their racist prank call. "Sure you will. Go right ahead." He had issued the challenge. Would I rise to it?

The following week, while I met with Norm to discuss the progress of my senior thesis, I told him what had happened. "What do you want to do about the incident?" he asked me. Good question.

The truth was, my threats to the frat boys were idle. I didn't think I had enough information on them, and I was sure nothing would come of me filing a complaint. Had they done anything horrible? Was asking me if I ate dogs enough to warrant a formal statement? Was pretending to speak in Vietnamese offensive enough to merit punishment? Whom would I even report them to? I mulled over these questions as Norm waited. I looked at him.

"Hong, what would you like the outcome to be in this situation?"

What *did* I want to have happen? I wasn't sure. Up to that point in my life, I had experienced mostly minor incidents that hinted at racism, but they were in no way physically harmful to me. I did my best not to let them get into my head. Instead, I spent most of my time trying to be like a duck and let those microaggressions glide off my back. The only time I had been physically threatened, my primary aggressor was another Vietnamese girl. Was I willing to file a formal complaint and get to the root of this issue with the frat guys?

In the midst of my thesis project, I was feeling a keen sense of responsibility to stand up for myself and the other Asian students I had met and interviewed. I didn't think I could let that Friday-night call slide. What would it say about me? Was I not willing to stand up to these guys and make them pay for what they'd done, even if they only viewed it as a joke? When would they learn that their jokes were hurtful and deeply rooted in racism?

After considering my options, Norm helped me file a report with the campus police. The information I had gleaned was enough to determine which fraternity the guys belonged to. When Norm told me that my complaint had resulted in the guys and the rest of their brothers being required to attend a sensitivity workshop to discuss racism and stereotypes, I still had mixed feelings. Had I made a mountain out of a molehill? Did they curse me as they sat through their workshop? I had insisted that my name be omitted from the formal police report, but I feared they would find me and physically harm me. I could only hope that whatever workshop they had to sit through would make some measure of difference in how they perceived and treated the Asian students on campus.

It was a step in the right direction, even if I didn't feel it at the time. In a way, I had marginally redeemed myself for being such a coward with Jeff and Dave. They had offended me, but it was unintentional, and they were friends, not drunk strangers pranking me on the phone late at night.

*   *   *

After donning my cap and gown at the commencement ceremony, I spent the summer finishing my thesis. I had to submit my project to Norm before I could officially graduate. With Norm's guidance, I went through several revisions before he accepted my thesis as complete. I'm not sure it was my best work, but at that time, it was the most extensive piece of writing I had done, and I was proud to have finished it.

With my time on campus over, I thanked Norm for his guidance, and I thanked Anne and Gunda for the employment and experience they had given me. I had left my job at the Bay Leaf by June of my final year to work at an optometrist's office in Kansas City, which made it easy to avoid running into Doug when he came home to visit his parents. I could go a bit longer without the embarrassment of revisiting unfamiliar jazz lyrics.

I had thought of applying to graduate school, but when my GRE score came back low in the spring, Norm asked me, in his ever-patient tone, "Have you thought about working for a while instead?" That was enough to knock the idea of graduate school down a few notches on my list of life goals.

My job as an optometrist's assistant in Kansas City paid better than my job at the Bay Leaf, but it didn't inspire me, and I decided not to stay on. By the time I finished college, I had lived a total of eight years in Kansas. I itched to get out and move on, feeling there was more to life and that I needed to go some-where, anywhere. I wanted to get away from my mom, to be an adult finally. I wanted to get away from my college town, afraid I would always want to be a college student if I stayed. My mother's younger brother, Tuyển, had moved from Wichita to Seattle some years before, and I decided I would do the same. I packed my bags and flew out to Washington State to start the next chapter in my life. I had a few boxes of worldly possessions and a few hundred dollars to my name. I wanted a new start in a new place. I wanted to leave behind the girl who didn't listen to jazz and wasn't good enough to date a college professor's son, the girl who had no confidence to speak up to her white friends about Lunar New Year. I wanted to try fitting into my skin better. I was ready to reinvent myself.

I settled into the spare bedroom of Uncle Tuyển's house in West Seattle as I searched for a job. Job searching was just as un-fun in Seattle as it had been in Kansas, and my BA in sociology *with honors* didn't take me very far. What does one do with a sociology degree, if not become a sociologist? My mother bad-gered me incessantly, calling to discuss—and by discuss, I mean lament—my career prospects. "I told you that worthless degree would get you nowhere! You should have studied to become a doctor." I resorted to avoiding her calls in order to dodge her nagging. She was persistent, however, and had Uncle Tuyển keep tabs on me. They meant well, but I did what many recent college graduates do—I believed myself smarter than I was.

I eventually accepted a position as the receptionist and office manager for a small optometrist's office situated at the back of a large optical store at Southcenter Mall. I had moved two time zones to the west, only to land nearly the same job I'd left be-hind. But I had student debt and a new car loan to pay back, and a job was a job. I made the best of the situation and got to know the doctors and technicians in the store.

A year after I started, I decided to move on. I wanted to

be around more people my age and went to work as a server at Applebee's. The restaurant was newly opened, and the fast pace was invigorating. I made friends with the staff, and we went camping, rafting, and hiking in our time off. Life had never been more aimless, yet more carefree.

It took another year before that got old, too.

Are You Lost, Dears?

By the summer of 1995, I was twenty-two and hardly the success I thought I would be, having so gloriously been the first in my family to finish college. I yearned for purpose and a sense of belonging in the world. Not just the yearning for cultural identity, but more as a citizen doing good. At the time, I wanted to do more than serve food and drinks. I wanted to make a mark in the world. I guess I figured the cultural stuff would eventually work itself out.

The Peace Corps intrigued me, but I had no passport or even a certificate of naturalization. I couldn't leave the United States, so when Maria, a friend from high school, told me about how she became a teacher, I listened. She learned of Teach For America (TFA) coming out of college and was now teaching third grade in Seattle. She had no teaching background and no certificate, but TFA hired her to teach in a disadvantaged school. A partner of AmeriCorps, the national service teaching network, TFA was founded on Wendy Kopp's plan to recruit liberal arts majors for tough-to-fill positions in economically hard-hit school districts.

The idea that I could teach poor children in poor schools appealed to my sense of seeking purpose. I had grown up poor.

I had lived in government housing. I knew what these kids were going through because I had been where they were. And if I could graduate from college and direct my own life's path at least a little, perhaps I could inspire them to do the same, too.

I applied, and despite botching my math lesson in the group interview, I was accepted into the program.

"Where's the Bay Area?" I asked the TFA staff person who called to inform me of my location assignment. I had never been to California. I thought she meant the Chesapeake Bay. She was probably thinking it was a mistake to hire me.

Most educators study and train for years before they walk into their own classroom. I had four weeks of training in Houston. TFA's summer training institute was a crash course in classroom management and lesson planning. It was hot and humid, but female trainees were required to wear pantyhose if wearing skirts or dresses. I opted for slacks. Training was a blur, although I remember planning simple classroom activities and teaching a group of summer school students. We were given guidelines and tips for gathering ideas and preparing lessons. This arsenal was meant to help us survive our two years of teaching. I often wondered why curriculum and materials weren't coming from the schools to which we would be assigned, but that was because I constantly forgot that we were in the trenches of education, teaching in long-forgotten schools with hardly any budget and not enough people who cared.

My first group consisted of third and fourth graders. There were Black students, Southeast Asian students, a few white students, one Samoan girl, a Chinese boy, and some Hispanic students. In all, I had thirty-five pupils that year.

Each student was unique and came to school with the baggage their young minds carried from home. Many of them had no structure or support, and the few who did kept quiet. As a class, they spoke over me, wandered around the classroom in the middle of lessons, and didn't hesitate to punch or kick one another. Though I taught them how to pronounce my last name (like "Win," not "Ung-guy-in"), most of them fell into the habit of calling me Miss Nu-yen.

"Miss Nu-yen, Jerome threw a pencil at me!"

"Miss Nu-yen, Landon won't shut up, and I can't concentrate with all his joking around!"

"Miss Nu-yen, Vu is feeding his Giga Pet again!"

"Miss Nu-yen, I need to go pee!"

It didn't matter that I was in the middle of a lesson, going over instructions for what they were to do next, or lining them up for recess. They were rowdy and lawless. It was hard to love them and even harder to teach them.

We muddled through the year with hand-me-down materials I cobbled together with the help of veteran teachers. Our school was on a year-round calendar, and given the shortage of space, my students and I took classrooms vacated by those who were on break for the month.

Just before Christmas, my classroom-management system had fallen apart, and I couldn't get the students to cooperate long enough to learn something, anything. In the middle of a writing exercise, they collectively decided they were done and started running around, talking louder and louder. "Quiet down, class!" I yelled. Maybe three of them heard me and sat down. The rest continued their conversations and antics. One of the runners tripped, and laughter erupted. I walked out of the portable class-room and stood at the door, watching through the window as the chaos went on unabated in my absence.

Frustrated with my lack of control and feeling ineffectual in my teaching efforts, I burst into tears. I had been so sure I could make a difference, that in me, these kids would see some-one who knew their personal struggles, who could relate to what their lives were like. But I was just another adult, a teacher, and an incredibly pathetic authority figure.

Minutes into my private pity party, my Samoan student's

mother walked by. Josefina was one of the few parents who volunteered at the school. I had welcomed her into my classroom
when she offered to come read with the students. She was a re-
liable presence when I needed to break the class up into smaller
groups.

Josefina took one look at my tear-streaked face and came
up the three steps from the pavement of the courtyard. "What
has happened, Miss Nguyen?" She pronounced my name "Win"
because, unlike the students, she remembered how I had first
introduced myself.

"The kids won't listen to me at all. Just look at them! I cannot get anything done with them like this." I pointed, and she
peered through the window to see paper airplanes and spitballs
flying through the air, three kids chasing one another between
the desks, a couple of girls drawing on the chalkboard. In the
back of the room, far from the door, two boys were standing on
their chairs, trying to pull down the posters I had put up to per-
sonalize the classroom so that it would feel like ours, if only for
four weeks.

Josefina clucked. Grabbing the doorknob, she yanked the
door open and stepped inside.

"Enough!" she bellowed in her loudest, sternest voice. She
wasn't much taller than me, and I was impressed by the authority
she exuded with just one word. "Everyone sit down!"

Every student froze in place, turned to see her standing at
the front of the room, and immediately scrambled for their seats.
Josefina's daughter, Talia, had been huddled with two other girls,
talking. Talia returned to her seat, pressed her lips together, and
lowered her eyes. One by one, the other students followed suit.

"Never have I seen such disrespectful students. Your behavior is unacceptable. Did any of you even notice your teacher has
walked out? Or is that why you decided to run around like a pack
of wild animals?"

I watched through the window as she scolded them. Those

who were near the front of the room were better positioned to see me standing outside. They at least looked contrite.

"I am going to leave now. Miss Nguyen will come back in, and she will continue her lessons with you. Show her the respect she deserves as your teacher. She works hard to make sure you learn what you need to know. If she reports to me that you are anything but respectful, I will have Mrs. Palmer come to chat with you. Do you need the principal sitting in here with you?"

Mrs. Sandra Palmer was not a principal any of the students wanted sitting next to them during lesson time. Sandra was well aware of my struggles as a new teacher and had routinely offered advice; she had also paired me up with two other veteran teachers who provided curriculum support and lesson ideas. She knew my students were a wild bunch, even by Oakland standards. While she was a congenial administrator to teachers and staff, her reputation among students was that of a strict disciplinarian who expected quiet lines in hallways, respectful words in conversation, and dedication to learning. She was nice, but her no-nonsense expectations were high.

I could have seen Josefina's scolding of the students as undermining my authority, but I knew that she meant well, and truthfully, I had little authority to begin with. Sucking in a breath and gathering my wits, I stepped back into the classroom, grabbed some tissues to wipe my eyes and blow my nose, and resumed my lessons.

My Vietnamese students came as a group to apologize to me at dismissal that afternoon. "We're sorry, Miss Nguyen. We will be better from now on."

It gave me hope that at least some of my students were empathetic to my struggles. Thankfully, the students never got that out of control again for the remainder of the year, and I managed not to cry in front of them when teaching became unbearable, which seemed like a weekly occurrence. More often than not, I felt there wasn't enough of me or of what they needed to help them with their problems. They did not have enough to eat. Their parents were abusive, not parenting enough, or parenting too much. Some of the kids wore dirty clothes—one student smelled like urine and feces most days. They had no pencils or paper at home to get homework done and no books to read. They witnessed drive-by shootings and other gang activities in their neighborhood. How could I expect them to focus on learning when they had such overwhelming burdens and problems on their minds?

One student, Felix, stood nearly six feet tall but was reading below grade level and missed school regularly. I pushed him to learn when he did come, but he threatened lawsuits when I gave low marks and disciplined him for fighting with other students.

My Chinese student, Samuel, was his scholastic opposite and a nemesis in and out of the classroom. Samuel was incredibly book smart but spent his free time antagonizing his classmates and me in the form of antics he felt were funny—sticking straws up his nose and knocking the math manipulatives off their tables. I learned early on that his father was strict and forbidding, so I kept him in check with a simple, "Do I need to call your dad?" In retrospect, using his father's abuse to manage Sam's classroom behavior was not one of my shining moments as a teacher. He was wound so tight at home, it was no mystery that he would let loose in the classroom.

Near the end of the school year, I mustered up my courage and agreed to take the class on a field trip with another teacher and her class. Samuel was playing with the other students when he ran into a taut cable anchoring a tree to the ground at a city park. The cable sliced his eyebrow, and we ended up in the emergency room. As Samuel and I waited for the school principal and his parents to arrive, Samuel cried, not from the bloody injury but from the anticipation of the beating his father was sure to give him when they got home. I felt helpless and so sorry for him. It was one of the few times that school year when I truly connected with one of my students.

Whereas Felix made idle threats about lawsuits, Samuel's father followed through and filed one against the school district and the city. "He's an unruly boy, and I can't keep him under control, but I have these hospital bills that someone ought to pay." Poor Samuel was simply stifled and longing for freedom. When the final bell rang on the last day of school, I thanked the Lord above for getting us through.

My second year of teaching was the antithesis of my first. I was given a group of first and second graders. There were twenty-five of them, and none was yet my height, an advantage in my favor. These students were sweet, were still eager to learn, and came to school each day with fresh energy for education. I decided right away to follow their lead. We studied Vincent van Gogh in depth, from his paintings to his personal struggles. I worried they were too young to know about depression and mental illness, but they came with maturity from their own challenges. "He was so sad, Miss Nguyen," Xuân said when I read to the students the story of Van Gogh cutting off his ear. "But I'm glad he was able to paint. Maybe that helped him not be so sad." I read aloud to them, and we discovered together how to add and subtract using tiny bears and yellow cubes.

The summer after my first year, I moved into an old Victorian house in West Oakland. My housemate, a fellow TFA teacher named Joe, and I were the only people in the neighborhood who weren't Black. "Are you lost, dears?" the ladies next door asked when they saw Joe and me on the sidewalk out front, waiting for our future landlord. There were no drugstores or grocery stores, and the nearest BART station was so unsavory, I was stuck walking home one night after getting off the train because no taxis would come for me. The neighborhood was neglected, but the street I lived on was lined with gingko trees, and the yards were well kept. Our neighbors couldn't decide if we were brave or crazy for renting the house, but the rent was cheaper than at our previous Lake Merritt apartment, and we had a big backyard with mature avocado and tangerine trees.

My first and second graders complained constantly of being hungry, so that winter, when the tangerines ripened, I picked the fruits I could reach without having to climb the tree and hauled them to school for the kids to snack on. We would take ten minutes each morning to break from our lessons and nourish our bodies. For some of my students, the tangerines were the only fresh fruit they ate. We savored the sweet, slightly tart wedges as they came away from the peel. I let the students serve themselves. The citrus scent would fill the classroom and perk us up for the remainder of our morning.

My adorable and eager-to-learn first- and second-grade students, 1998

The main reason TFA assigned me to the Bay Area was that there was an initiative at the time to educate the students in their native languages, whether it was Vietnamese or the controversial Ebonics. I was charged with leading a classroom where one-third of my students were Vietnamese. My aide was an older Vietnamese man named Mr. Đỗ, who pulled the students aside to give them Vietnamese-language lessons. Whether he was also tasked with helping the other students, I was never clear. Though I had grown up learning to speak, read, and write in Vietnamese, I rarely used it outside of my family. Mostly because I never learned the vocabulary to speak regularly to outsiders. I rarely spoke in Vietnamese to my Vietnamese students or to Mr. Đỗ. I deferred to him to teach them to read and write in Vietnamese, but once I was called on by their parents to draw the line when he taught them a song that was deemed sympathetic to the Communist regime.

* * *

I was in my mid-twenties and in the middle of my two-year TFA commitment in Oakland when I decided to apply to law school. I had thought teaching would provide me with a clear path and a meaningful career, but the district's internal conflicts and the challenges of inner-city life chipped away at my optimism. I figured the best way to help people and make lots of money was to get into law. I studied for the LSAT on my days off and researched schools back in Seattle, where I had maintained residency. I watched too many episodes of *Ally McBeal* and imagined my career would be filled with short-skirted suits and after-work drinks. I wouldn't sing, though, because I can't sing to save my life.

In my application to the University of Washington School of Law, I was required to include a personal statement. I needed to distinguish myself from other applicants and convince the admissions committee of the value I would add to the school's student population. In that vein, I drafted a statement that painted a picture of a poor girl from a large immigrant family:

> I'm one of seven children . . . I was raised by a
> single mother, a woman widowed in her early
> thirties when her husband, a hardworking fish-
> erman, died suddenly . . . I was the first in my
> family to graduate from college. We were ref-
> ugees of the Vietnam War. We are immigrants
> . . . I grew up knowing poverty . . . I want to
> study law so that I can represent others who are
> disadvantaged.

Oh, it was a bleak, grim piece. I spoke of how difficult it was to achieve my goals in the face of financial straits, to rise above my lot in life with everything being against me. I played up the gender, race, economic, and social aspects of my life to gain acceptance to law school. I believed that my position as one of society's underdogs would make the admissions committee feel sorry for me, that they would allow me a spot in the incoming class. If I couldn't be one of the school's many affluent students, I would stand out among those who were poor.

At orientation on my first day of law school, we gathered in the big theater-style classroom to hear what the professors had to say, to gather strength and encouragement, to be reminded that a legal education was not an easy one. As I looked around me, I counted the number of Asian women I would study along-side. There were more than a dozen of us out of about 150 students. *Huh.*

Nancy, Yoko, Jen, Cat, Abby, Marinel, and Joeana were some of the women I saw during orientation. They were Korean, Filipina, and Japanese Americans. It turned out I was one of many college-educated, accomplished Asian American women in that class who would eventually graduate from UW law school. I had been silly to believe my story about being a dirt-poor disadvantaged student was a plus, still playing the victim when my peers were already envisioning their law careers. At the age of twenty-five, I hadn't learned that my story was also that of many others. So what if I was an immigrant? So what if I was poor? So what if I was raised by a single parent? Now, as I embarked on three utterly miserable years of law school, I was finally seeing and understanding that I was not alone. All my years of trying to fit in, of denying my ethnicity, of wanting to be anyone other than myself were coming to an end. Looking around at all these other Asian women, looking at the Black and Hispanic students, looking at the other minorities in that room, my outlook shifted. This was the beginning of a different journey for me, one of acceptance and acknowledgment. One that was long overdue.

And I wasn't sure I was equipped to handle it.

* * *

Until the spring of 1988, my mom; older brother, Cường; older sister, Hà; younger sister, Hạnh; and I were all resident aliens permanently living in the United States. Mom wanted to visit Pope John Paul II at the Vatican but didn't have a passport to travel, so she applied to become a US citizen. Cường, Hạnh, and I were still minors and fell under Mom's application. Hà was over eighteen and had to apply for citizenship separately, so she and our mother both received their certificates of naturalization at that time.

Cường, Hạnh, and I had not received documentation of our new status.

"Do I get a certificate?" I had asked. "And what about Cường and Hạnh?"

"You're a citizen now," Mom told me. "Just do the paperwork when you're older, and they'll give you yours. My friend said it will be easy." The truth, it turned out, was that Mom couldn't afford to do the paperwork to get our certificates. She had just enough to pay for herself and our older sister.

They both changed their names. I envied their name changes and looked forward to the day when I could get myself a new name. I needed to come up with a shortlist for when my time came.

The problem with my application at the age of twenty-five was that having gained citizenship as a minor, I didn't need to reapply—I was already a citizen; I just didn't have the certificate saying I was. While teaching in Oakland, I decided I wanted to see more of the world. That required a passport, which required proof of citizenship. When I researched which forms to complete, I ran into trouble. The agents at the immigration office in San Francisco had a difficult time directing me to the correct process because they weren't sure, either. Did I need a replacement certificate? Or did I need to apply for naturalization? It was complicated and not at all simple, as Mom's friend had promised.

A month into law school, I received an interview notice from the immigration office in San Francisco. It was the appointment I had been waiting to get for over a year. I hastily booked flights from Seattle and skipped two days of classes. I would not miss this for anything.

"Hong New-yen?" a tall Black woman called from her position in the doorway.

"Yes!" I ejected myself from my waiting room seat, nervous and excited about this interview.

I don't remember the agent's name. Her office was a tight box with a desk piled high with case files. My folder was open on her desk, and I could see the little photos of myself I had submitted with my application. The agent picked up a piece of paper that I couldn't quite make out and slotted it into the typewriter.

"Please state and spell your full name."

"Hong Thi Thu Nguyen," I said, then spelled out each part of my name.

She asked for my date of birth, place of birth, and my parents' names. Sometimes she clacked on the typewriter; other times, she simply scrutinized me from across the desk. My palms were damp. I stuck my hands under my thighs to keep from fidgeting. This was such an unusual interview.

"Do you want to change your name?"

"Yes."

"What would you like to change it to?"

I never did get around to making that shortlist of names I liked. "Do I need to give you my new name now?"

"Yes, I need to put it on your certificate."

"You mean I'm getting my certificate?" I must have sounded like an idiot.

"That's why you're here, isn't it?"

"I thought this was just an interview to go over my application," I told her.

"This is not an interview. See here? I'm typing up your certificate. Now, what would you like your new name to be?"

Gah! I couldn't think of any names at that moment. This was going to be my name for the rest of my life. It had to be good and well thought-out.

"I haven't given it any thought."

"You want to keep your old name, then? You can always change it later."

I didn't think she would appreciate me asking for a few minutes to consider names. "I guess I'll keep my name for now." I felt myself deflating in the hard metal chair.

Clack. Clack. Clack. She completed typing and pulled the document out of her machine. "OK, hold up your right hand and repeat after me."

I repeated an oath to be loyal to the United States of America, my home and country of citizenship. I swore off any loyalty to Việt Nam, which I wasn't sure I had a whole lot of anyway. The entire process took about fifteen minutes. I signed my certificate.

There was no ceremony. I had no friends or family with me to mark the occasion. This was not at all how I had thought it would be. Where was the room full of people? The photo ops, flags on the stage, and chorus of voices declaring our shared love for the land of the free, home of the brave? It was just the two of us, this nameless immigration agent and me. She shook my hand and gave me my certificate of naturalization.

"Don't lose this document," she cautioned. "It's your original certificate and proof that you're an American."

Without a birth certificate, doing normal things like getting my driver's license, enrolling in school, and applying for jobs had been filled with extra steps. Over the years, I'd had to submit notarized affidavits stating that I was who I was. I constantly had to explain why I lacked the legal documents to prove I was a living and breathing member of society. My alien registration card was never enough.

I carefully tucked the certificate into my folder and thanked the agent before exiting her office and the building. The sounds of traffic and bustling sidewalks greeted me as I stepped out into the crisp fall afternoon. It was October 1998, and I was finally a certificate-carrying naturalized American citizen.

You Are Vietnamese If . . .

During the summer after my second year of law school, I was in Los Angeles working as an intern at a public-interest law firm, focusing on children's rights, adoption, and guardianship cases. As a legal advocate and a champion for the disadvantaged, I was proud of my achievements. I had finally moved up the ranks. I was no longer the victim. I was someone helping the victim.

Thúy-Lan, a Vietnamese girl I had met in junior high school and one of the recently arrived refugees I'd befriended back then, included me in a list of recipients of an email she'd found to be funny. Thúy-Lan and I had been good friends but drifted apart after moving on to different high schools, so we hadn't been in regular contact. I was curious to see her name pop up in my email inbox.

The email was a list of stereotypes about Asians. It was meant to be a joke, poking fun at accents, love for certain foods, how they handled finances. The list was extensive. I say "they" because I had worked long and hard to dissociate myself from the Vietnamese and other Asians around me. I was Vietnamese but NOT. I was Asian but NOT. I was American.

I read the stereotypes slowly. I've corrected punctuation, spelling, and formatting errors, but these are the stereotypes as I received them in that email:

Subject: Re: If you are confused of who you are, here is the checklist:

YOU ARE CHINESE IF . . .
1. You think you're the smartest people in the world.
2. You have a pager and cellular phone with you at all the time.
3. You and 2 other guys talking, people think you are fighting.
4. Today's steamed rice is tomorrow's fried rice.
5. Dim Sum is your breakfast.
6. Noodle is your dinner.
7. You don't like eating FISH.
8. Most member in your family wearing denture at young age.
9. Your most favorite color is RED.
10. You're afraid of black people.
11. You think you are superior to all other Asians.

YOU ARE JAPANESE IF . . .
1. You're obsessed with your hair, your car, and your clothes.
2. You want to marry a Korean American or Chinese American woman (males) or you want to marry a white guy (females).
3. You are extremely polite and acting innocent.
4. Your feet look funny in the way you walk.

5. You're afraid of black people.
6. You think you are superior to all other Asians.

YOU ARE KOREAN IF . . .

1. You smoke and drink too much.
2. You will die instantly if you stop drinking Soju and eating Kimchi.
3. You spend more time in the bar than at home.
4. You either drive a Hyundai or Mercedes.
5. You can play piano.
6. You're actually sorry that Margaret Cho's sitcom was canceled.
7. You're afraid of black people.
8. You only conduct business with your local Korean business.
9. You speak Korean in 99.9% of your time on social occasions.
10. You have at least one relative who owns a liquor store.
11. You think you are superior to all other Asians.

YOU ARE FILIPINO IF . . .

1. You want to be a dancer, a singer, or an actor, even though you have a day job as a nurse, a security guard, a dishwasher, a waiter/waitress, or an accountant.
2. You keep telling everyone that a member of your family back home is a politician or a movie star.
3. You brought lots of dried fishes when coming back from vacation in Philippines.

4. You like wearing GOLD on your ear, neck, hands, and fingers.
5. At least one member of your family is a nurse.
6. Your sister or daughter marries a US military serviceman.
7. There are 20 people sharing rooms in your home.
8. You have at least 2 FULL-TIME jobs.
9. You're not afraid of black people; in fact, you wish you were black.
10. You don't care if you are superior to all other Asians.

YOU ARE CAMBODIAN IF . . .
1. Your family has a Donut shop.
2. You eat smelly perished catfish.
3. You know well about some sort of invisible spirit and power.
4. You are good at cursing people to make them sick or die.

YOU ARE INDIAN IF . . .
1. Your uncle is some kind of Doctor.
2. Your brothers and you are some kind of Computer Engineer.
3. Your Mom and Pop own a motel, Seven Eleven, or Gas Station.
4. You hate to spend money.

YOU ARE VIETNAMESE IF . . .
1. You've gotta have fish sauce with every meal.
2. You spend so much time in topless, bikini coffee shops and in Quan Nhau (pubs).

3. If you don't get Pho, you will die sooner or later.
4. You and your family care about Education and at least you guys try to do something about it.
5. Someone in your family is in Nails/Hair/Taxis/Fishing business or in clothing business.
6. You drive a brand-new Lexus or Acura or Toyota 4Runner.
7. You carry a big box of instant noodle in your car trunk.
8. You shop at 99c [sic] stores, flea markets, K-Mart, Costco, Ross and Marshall.
9. You have banana, chili or all kind of veggies in your backyard.
10. You add more rooms to rent for extra income.
11. Your favorite beer is Heineken.
12. Your favorite speakers are JBL and Bose.
13. Most of you guys have a Karaoke system and a big screen Sony in your family room.
14. You never think of traveling on First Class in your life.
15. Your Mom has special taste about jewelry & real estate.
16. Someone in your family is on some kind of welfare.
17. You prefer using cash rather than check or credit card.
18. You care about politics but do nothing about it.
19. You hate being mixed with other Asian guys.
20. You don't like to have a Vietnamese look.
21. You don't like other Vietnamese guys either.

22. You are not afraid of black people or any
    kind of people.
23. You can make more money with less time
    and effort than other Asian guys.

I was livid. I stewed in my rage and then wrote a reply to everyone on that message: *This is the exact kind of shit that allows crazy stereotypes and poor English skills to get perpetuated among Asians. Do not respond to me (Hong) if you're offended by what I'm saying; I'm only saying it like it is.*

I didn't start with a salutation, and I didn't end with a closing or my name. I didn't believe anyone who found the stereotypes amusing deserved an ounce of civility. I was blind with rage for the insults, accusations, and blanket assumptions. I was angry at Thúy-Lan for sending the message, thinking it was funny, and perpetuating the stereotypes that were laid bare. I thought back to when we had started drifting apart.

"I don't like going over there," she had said on the phone when I called to invite her to my house. It was the summer after our ninth-grade year together. "Your mom is always cooking, and your house stinks. I don't want that smell to get on my clothes." Her words stung. The inner conflict I felt as a thirteen-year-old percolated, and I realized I had used Thúy-Lan's remarks to effectively nudge myself in the direction of keeping my distance from other Asians in high school. If my Vietnamese friend couldn't stand how we smelled, what was everyone else thinking? She had given me an opening for rejecting our shared heritage, and I willingly took it. I spent years hiding myself, yet here she was laughing at our collective foibles, and I was the one upset. Was she embracing these stereotypes? Which side of the fence was she on? Which side was I on?

Over the years since I had last seen Thúy-Lan, I'd studied race and culture in my sociology courses. After college, I continued to read books, researched Asian American history, and visited museums to learn and see what I had turned my back on. I was trying hard to understand people of not just my own culture but of other cultures, too. I digested the contents of her email, recognizing that I was only in the infancy of accepting myself as I was. I still hesitated to give up my invisibility, so ingrained was the idea that to be American, I had to blend in. I allowed myself to be Asian, but I knew I still had to be relatable to non-Asians.

I could not comprehend why anyone would pass around such inflammatory statements, claiming they were just a joke. And what made it worse was that from the bad grammar of the author, I was certain that he or she was likely one of the many Asians being disparaged. I was angry that Asians would be shamed and put down by one of their own. This email was a wake-up call for me to stand up for myself and for everyone else being victimized for our ethnicity.

Thúy-Lan responded to my email blast:

> I'm the one responsible for this. The people on
> the list are my good friends, just like you are.
> Your expressing of your opinion shows how
> opinionated you are and how unfamiliar you are
> of the VN community, not to mention you're
> embarrassing/insulting ME. I'm sure you know
> the email etiquettes . . . We all have our opin-
> ions. I'll express them when I know all the facts
> and nature of the situation. In this case, it's
> simply just a joke. I'm going to send out anoth-
> er email to the same group telling them that the
> email was just a joke and I apologize if I offend
> anyone. Your name will again be on the list, but
> only for the last time.

Despite saying she would include me in her group response, Thúy-Lan's direct reply was the last time I heard from her. My mom ran into her about a year later, and they spoke cordially. When Mom asked me during one of my rare visits home why Thúy-Lan and I no longer kept in touch, I shrugged. I'm not sure my mother ever understood my identity crisis, and I didn't feel I could adequately express to her how I had felt my entire life, nor did I care to. It was not a discussion I was ready to engage in with her or anyone else.

* * *

By my final months of law school, I had long given up the idea that I would practice law. I didn't want to be adversarial every day, to argue for a living. I didn't have a clue what I was going to do once I graduated, but at that point, I wanted to feed my creative self, so I took a course called Law, Literature and Film, a welcome departure from the required courses—Contracts, Torts, Criminal Procedure, and my least favorite, Secured Transactions (got a D). In the film class, the professor, with his quiet voice and salt-and-pepper beard, led us in discussions about how the law and legal aspects of life played out in stories, television shows, and movies. It was a small roundtable setting, and we were encouraged to speak freely about our perspectives and feelings on the topics covered, which included racism and culture.

One assigned book was *Donald Duk*, a coming-of-age novel written by Frank Chin. Donald Duk is an eleven-year-old boy dealing with the struggles of cultural identity. Donald is American-born but has trouble finding the balance between accepting the American aspects of his life and those of his Chinese heritage. Donald feels that his family rejects American culture even though they live in America. After he learns about the role of Chinese immigrants in the building of railroads in America,

Donald finds himself viewing white people as racist for not giving credit to the Chinese for their contributions.

I read the book and mulled over the author's message. I saw myself in Donald in the ways he tried to erase his ethnic heritage. I was that boy, acting out to reject my Vietnamese identity, to actively embrace only my American self.

I had learned about the Vietnam War in school, but only superficially, and my main takeaway was that a great number of American soldiers died for a country that wasn't their own. I felt guilty for being a part of it—that somehow, it was my fault or that of my family's. Over the years, veterans I met had told me they fought in 'Nam. I never knew how to respond. Was I supposed to say thank you? None of my history classes included lessons about the when, why, and how of my people leaving our homeland with little more than the clothes on our backs. Until I started looking for stories about the war and how the Vietnamese came to America, I was ignorant of how we ended up in the United States. It was not a topic we discussed at home; my parents were too busy trying to survive to dwell on the past.

As I sat in the roundtable discussion about *Donald Duk*, I listened to what my classmates had to say. They found this or that interesting. Their statements were light and easy to digest. Feeling safe and suddenly in the mood to share, I decided to speak up.

"I didn't know there were Asians in America before the Vietnam War," I confessed in a quivering voice, recalling what I learned in my American Studies courses. "Until I was in college, I didn't know that Chinese immigrants built the railroads or that the US government put Japanese Americans into concentration camps during World War II."

I looked around the conference table at the faces of my white, Black, and Asian classmates. Young, old. They were from small and large cities. It was a diverse group. Those who had been whispering to one another stopped speaking and looked at me. The ones who heard me looked confused, amused even. Some seemed to be in disbelief. I forged on.

"I didn't know anything about Asians in America, and I can relate to Donald because I've spent many years trying to scrub myself of being Vietnamese."

Tears formed as I looked at Michael Lau, a handsome mixed-race Asian student I had gotten to know. He looked back at me with concern and pity. We had met at some point in law school and spoke often. He and I talked about our coursework, our interests, our futures, but we never talked much about being Asian. He had traveled and lived abroad. He'd graduated from Notre Dame and Stanford. After law school, he was bound for the big time. I felt as if we were opposites.

Here I was, a student in a top-notch program, and I had suddenly turned my law school classroom into a therapist's office by revealing the depths of my shortcomings and ignorance. I sat at that table facing my peers, feeling as if this admission was my stamp of stupidity, while hot tears streaked down my cheeks. I had scratched open the scab of my identity crisis and laid my wound open and raw to my professor and classmates. I don't recall if there was more to the discussion, but I was glad that time soon ran out and class ended. I packed up my books to leave, eyes puffy and cheeks taut from dried tears. To my surprise, Michael and another student, a Chinese American named Brad Li, approached me in the corridor. They hugged me and patted my back, and we left together.

As I recount this, tears have sprung up again. I can still feel the shame and ignorance of the ethnicity-denying young woman I had been. I feel very much that this admission marked the final shedding of the American Only/No Vietnamese shell under which I had been hiding. I believe that in their hugs and pats, Michael and Brad were acknowledging our common struggle, and they were willing to forgive me, us, for our faults as we sought out where we belonged in this world. I was finally getting past the ways I had contorted myself to fit the mold for what I thought it meant to be American. I could move on with an unfamiliar and new sense of willingness and pride in owning who I was and who Asians were—and are—in America.

Returning to My ~~Motherland~~ Mother's Land

In 2001, my mom decided it was due time to visit Việt Nam, the country we had fled at the end of the war twenty-six years before. Having just graduated from law school and finding myself unemployed, I figured it was as good a time as any to go. I was nearing thirty and had yet to see where I was from. I had only been to Europe with a friend during law school, and I was desperate to get new stamps in my passport.

Going with my mom felt like the safe way to travel to Việt Nam. I would have been intimidated to go on my own, fearing that I didn't know enough Vietnamese to get around and that I would be taken advantage of or, worse, put into a reeducation camp. On a more spiritual level, I wanted to find the place where I belonged. I had spent my entire life not quite feeling like an American and yet not quite like a Vietnamese, either. I expected the trip to offer a sense of homecoming, and I thought that I would have a deep, soul-affirming transformation of myself into someone no longer questioning her identity.

On this trip, my companions were my mother, her two sisters

(Big Aunt—so named because she's the oldest of my mom's siblings—and Aunt Kim Liên), and Aunt Kim Liên's two children. Tim and Cecelia were in grade school then, so age-wise, I was caught in the middle, sort of an adult but not quite as adult as my mom and my aunts.

I expected that we would tour some historical sites and visit where they had lived, where my older siblings and I were born, where my mom and aunts went to school or got married, stuff like that. We would go to the beach, swim in the ocean, and get cheap massages in our free time. I was still living with my aunts after graduating from law school, biding my time before I would move to Hawaii in the winter. In preparation for our trip, Big Aunt and Aunt Kim Liên made frequent trips to the Goodwill on the edge of downtown Seattle, picking up clothes, shoes, linens, and whatever else looked good to give away to family and friends we were to meet "back home."

"You've gone again today?" I asked when I arrived home to find them opening new bags.

"Yes, and tomorrow there will be 25 percent off green tags, so we're going to go again. Do you want to come with us?" Aunt Kim Liên took this task seriously. I was astonished by their fervor each time they brought mountains of Goodwill bags through the door and piled them in the front room next to the baby grand piano. There were perfectly decent, second-hand, American-standard, high-quality clothes at rock-bottom prices to be bought for our distant relatives and the folks in their villages, and my aunts were making sure they would bring with us as much as the airlines would allow. As *Việt Kiều* (Vietnamese living outside of Việt Nam), we were deemed wealthy by those who remained in our native land or could not emigrate at the end of the Vietnam War, and we were expected to share some of our wealth. It would be shameful to show up without proper gifts and offerings to all those who were left behind and suffering.

My aunts shopped daily and packed the Goodwill items in large cardboard boxes, along with odds and ends like packs of glue sticks. The airlines we were flying had a limit of seventy pounds per box, and so Aunt Kim Liên and Big Aunt would take turns hefting the boxes onto the bathroom scale to determine how much more they could cram in.

"What does it say?" the one lifting would grunt. "Sixty-nine point five pounds," the other would reply after getting down on the floor to peer at the numbers on the scale. They had no business lifting such heavy boxes, and they really should have invested in a proper commercial scale. I ended up helping, but after three years of studying case law, I was not cut out for physical exertion, either.

As the boxes reached their weight limit, we applied rolls and rolls of clear packing tape over the surface of each box, around the sides, and along the seams, then covered them in metal-gray duct tape and, finally, once again in clear packing tape. Sometimes we would switch to the packing tape with filament reinforcement. One could not be too careful in one's packing of boxes for checked luggage. *There is no way the boxes will get damaged in transit with that much tape,* we all thought as we admired our handiwork.

On a clear and sunny day in early August, my aunts, cousins, and I flew out of Seattle into Vancouver, then on to Hong Kong, where we met my mom, who had traveled from Kansas. From Hong Kong, we would fly into Hà Nội together. Despite having checked in several maximum-weight boxes, we ourselves traveled lightly, each of us only carrying one small suitcase. I feared getting sunburned and diarrhea on this trip, so I packed sunblock and Imodium. I had no reason to worry about exceeding liquid allowances in my carry-on; we had yet to witness 9/11, and the rules were relaxed then.

Bleary-eyed from more than a day of flying and transiting, we landed in Hà Nội on the morning of August 4, 2001. It was drizzling and the sky was gray as we deplaned and were shuttled to the terminal for passport control clearance. The Noi Bai International Airport was aged, the sun having bleached the dark-blue paint to a chalky gray-blue. As there was no system of queuing up, we crowded together with the other travelers like sardines, waiting for our turn with the agent.

On the wall ahead of us were two signs, one in Vietnamese and its counterpart in English.

In Vietnamese: *Line up in an orderly fashion. Present your passport and entry form to the agent. No money allowed to change hands.*

In English: *Line up in an orderly fashion. Present your passport and entry form to the agent. No other papers allowed to change hands.*

I was fluent in English and knew enough Vietnamese that I was certain I had made no mistake in my reading of the signs. I suspected there was something to the discrepancy.

When we finally reached the front, the agent took our US passports and entry forms and looked at each of us in turn. It was not difficult to discern we were Vietnamese Americans; our plump, pale faces gave us away, along with our Vietnamese names and birthplace notations in our passports. Name: Hong Thi Thu Nguyen. Place of Birth: Vietnam.

"Hmmm. Your forms are incorrect. There is a problem," the agent said to us in Vietnamese, frowning at our papers, barely looking up.

Aunt Kim Liên took the lead. "What's the problem?" she asked politely in Vietnamese.

"I don't know. Just something is wrong. Wait over there," the agent responded, pointing to the side of the counter. We shuffled over with our suitcases, backpacks, and purses. Other passengers were being ushered through, mostly locals and a few from other Asian countries.

"What's the problem?" Mom and Big Aunt wanted to know and fully expected their younger sister to have the answer.

"There's nothing wrong with our documents," I insisted to Aunt Kim Liên. I had looked them over before we landed.

"She's waiting for a bribe," Aunt Kim Liên said to Mom and Big Aunt in Vietnamese.

We all looked at one another. My cousins, too young and tired to tune into our dilemma, hung on to their suitcases for support behind me. I understood completely, but my sense of fairness rebelled. "That's ridiculous! She should let us in," I complained in English.

But clearly, we were not going anywhere unless we engaged the influence of crisp American dollar bills. We stood for another fifteen minutes as Aunt Kim Liên debated with her sisters over how much to offer. Finally, she slipped some bills into her passport, and we all shuffled back to the agent. "I think we have worked out what was wrong with our forms," my aunt said as she handed our bundle of documents to the agent. I frowned at the injustice of it, the corruption that we were faced with just as we stepped off the plane. Our forms were not quite right until Aunt Kim Liên's wallet was $65 lighter and the agent's pocket the equivalent of over a million in *đồng Việt* heavier.

No money allowed to change hands. Indeed.

Granted passage, we made our way to the baggage claim area. I looked across the way to the carousel and saw loose articles of clothing hanging from one of our boxes and other items—a shirt here, a pair of pants there—making their own way along the belt.

Oh shit. Our boxes had not traveled well. Apparently, much more tape was needed. And rope. *And proper suitcases instead of cardboard boxes, come to think of it.*

We rushed over and grabbed the loose articles of clothing

and busted boxes off the belt. We had brought a lot, and it was all hanging out for the world to see. There was no shortage of onlookers for our Vomiting Checked Baggage drama. During the frantic gathering of our wandering contents, we managed to locate our welcome committee—three uncles, three aunts, and three cousins who had come to greet us and deliver us safely to their home on the outskirts of Hà Nội. I had no idea they even existed—we had always been told that the only relatives left in Việt Nam were our paternal grandfather and, until she left, Aunt Kim Liên. *Interesting. Is this a skeleton in our family's closet?* Big Aunt immediately started crying upon sighting them. It would seem they were not strangers to her and she had been expecting this long-overdue reunion.

When introductions were made, I defaulted to simply calling everyone *cô* (aunt) and *chú* (uncle), a safe way to address people you do not know in Việt Nam. The Vietnamese are particular about titles, and I was biding my time until I could pull my mom aside for a quick rundown of who was who and what to call them. We all stood awkwardly on the pavement, making preliminary inquiries as to health and our respective trips as we waited for the driver to bring the vehicle around. I was hardly able to breathe in the thick, humid air, and my hair stuck to my face and neck.

Finally, we managed to load twenty boxes, six suitcases, our various backpacks and purses, and fifteen people plus our driver into a minibus meant to hold no more than twelve. Our welcome committee had come by intercity bus in advance of our arrival, and their belongings went into the minibus alongside ours. Then we made our way to the countryside. The vehicle's suspension could hardly support us, and our excessive weight kept us from going any faster than about forty miles an hour.

"How long will we be on the road?" I asked in Vietnamese, trying my best to sound polite and not as tired as I truly felt.

"We'll be there in a couple of hours," the driver replied. I looked happily out the window as we went along, answering questions my aunts and uncles peppered me with during the drive.

"Whose child are you? What is your name? Are you the oldest? Oh! You're the lawyer! But you look about eighteen years old." This line of querying was repeated as they each took their turn for two and a half hours. Each time I replied, I became more practiced in my answers in Vietnamese (yay, me!), but I also grew increasingly weary from the repetitive litany of questions and exclamations. At intervals, one or another would turn to me and ask, "Shouldn't you be married by now?"

When everyone tired of conversation, I watched the passing scenery. Tall stacks of white plastic patio chairs on motorbikes. Trucks full of chickens poking their beaks out of air holes. Trucks carrying pigs, with their rumps and curly tails jutting from wicker baskets. Entire families on creaky bicycles. I needed to take pictures of it all, but they flew past us too fast for my camera to capture. How fun, charming, and extraordinarily rustic. We were definitely not in America anymore.

The "couple of hours" turned into five. The roads were teeming with oxen, chickens, dogs, cats, motorbikes, mopeds, bicycles, pedestrians, cars, buses, vans, and commercial trucks. Despite the driver's incessant horn-honking ("I have to let the others know I'm behind them, next to them, passing them"), I eventually nodded off, exhausted. I napped, woke up to check on our progress, and napped again. There were only so many plump pink pigs and stacks of plastic chairs I really wanted to marvel at.

*   *   *

When at long last we pulled up in front of a house that we would call home for the next several days, there was not much chatter, only the unfurling of limbs in an effort to exit the minibus and drag ourselves inside. We were in Đông Xuyên, a quiet little village in Bắc Ninh, a province only twenty-five kilometers from the airport in Hà Nội. If any of us felt excitement about having arrived, we were too weary from our long journey to show it. I was just relieved to be out of the cramped minibus and done with the constant jostling from hitting potholes.

The matron of the household was the eldest sister of Big Aunt, Aunt Kim Liên, and my mother. How had my siblings and I never known of her? Aunt Hai was widowed and had two daughters and a son. It was a muddled introduction, and though her children were introduced as my cousins, it took constant internal reminders for me to avoid calling them *cô* and *chú*. It was as if no one really wanted to fully explain what had happened all those decades ago, to have Aunt Hai disappear from the family tree, only to reappear with grown children and no husband, living a quiet life in the countryside. I discovered the truth years later: she was not believed by my maternal grandfather to be his child, so he made no claim of her. *Brutal.* At least her sisters were willing to accept her in the family.

Their house was a boxy structure two stories high, constructed of gray cinder blocks and painted a bright yellow-green on the front but left bare on the sides and back. The main part of the house included a sitting room, a kitchen, and an open loft upstairs. The kitchen along the back wall was merely a vinyl countertop with a sink and a couple of hot plates for a stove, like those portable burners you would take to the beach or car camping if you knew there was an electrical outlet to plug them into. The kitchen didn't have a refrigerator, but I saw a small box television and a VCR in their sitting room. They could not keep food or drinks cold, but they could watch Vietnamese soap operas, movies, and concerts. I wondered at their priorities and wished for a tall glass of ice water. It was so hot and muggy, even with all the windows open and covered with sheer curtains that occasionally fluttered as the gentle breeze and flies came through.

The family normally slept upstairs in the loft, but in a show of hospitality and generosity, they insisted that we take the loft. Up the open stairs along the right wall in the sitting room we went. Where were the rails? I prayed the entire time that I would not lose my balance and fall over.

We dropped our suitcases and bags and returned downstairs to find the boxes being hauled in from the minibus. I imagined myself in a cool, misty shower, washing away all the grime from traveling. I would soap up my body and lather up the shampoo in my hair before rinsing myself thoroughly with copious amounts of refreshing water. I thought about which clean shirt and pants I would put on to replace my sweat-stained blouse and dusty jeans. I would pull my hair up into a clip to let my neck breathe as I laid down for a long, quiet nap on a soft bed.

Instead of doing any of that, we plopped down on the rugs in the sitting room and started sorting through the contents of all those boxes. I enjoyed it about as much as I would enjoy getting a cavity filled at the dentist. Shirts, shoes, pants, and everything else ended up in piles on the floor. It was a sea of clothing and school supplies, dotted here and there with my aunts, cousins, mother, and our hosts. The air was humid, and flies buzzed around us. I sat there wondering why I even needed to participate. Then it struck me that I could just excuse myself, which I did, then headed up to the loft.

Before I could get situated, someone down below suggested that we go out to meet my grandmother's older brother, whom everyone called Ông Cụ (the respectful way to address an elderly man), and to see the local church. This would be the first of dozens of churches on this trip, but I didn't know it then.

Dog Meat Served Here!

Ông Cụ's home was a short walk down the dirt road. My skin prickled in the heat as we made our way, and I could feel my clothes sticking to me and making me itch. I scratched the back of my neck under my hair, moving my sun hat around as I did so. I felt dizzy from all the hours we had spent on the planes and then in the minibus.

My youngest host cousin, Hoa, and I walked much faster than the rest of the group and reached the house first. "Hello!" she hollered as we entered without knocking.

"This is Hồng," she said, introducing me to Ông Cụ.

"Hello, Ông Cụ," I said with a slight bow to my head.

"Hello, granddaughter," he replied, adding, "I'm sorry, I cannot hear so well."

"It's not a problem," I said back. Then, "I'm sorry, my Vietnamese is not so good."

We smiled sheepishly at one another, his gummy grin to my gleaming-white toothy one. We spoke of the heat and our trip as we waited for everyone else to arrive.

"Where are the others?" he asked me when we ran out of topics.

"They walked slower than we did, so they should be here shortly," I told him. When I informed him of the members of the group, Ông Cụ piqued my interest, saying that he remembered Aunt Kim Liên very well.

"She was originally supposed to marry a young man, but he went off and married someone else, and then she left for the United States in 1977, still single." Aunt Kim Liên had always been my favorite aunt because we could easily communicate in English, and she had such a broad range of employable skills—as a kid, I wanted to grow up to be just like her. I thought I knew her well, but she had never told me about any previous love interests. I wondered what other secrets she kept. This trip was turning up all sorts of juicy family tidbits.

"She ended up getting married?" he asked.

"Oh yes, Ông Cụ," I replied. "She married and has two kids. They're with us, and you'll meet them when they get here." I figured he didn't need to know Aunt Kim Liên had been divorced for some years now.

The group arrived and bustled into the house. We stayed long enough for introductions and a couple more stories before excusing ourselves and saying farewell to Ông Cụ. From his house, we took a short walk down the road to the church. Outside the chapel, Mom insisted we stop for a photo in front of the statue of Saint Joseph. Mom, Big Aunt, and Aunt Kim Liên were big fans of the Virgin Mary and all the saints and could not pass up a photo op.

"It's been updated," Hoa told me before we walked into the main chapel.

I expected an old ramshackle structure with a musty and dark interior, but this church was unlike any I had ever seen. The outside was solidly constructed and finished. Where the exterior was modest, the interior was ornate. Eight crimson columns, four on each side, rose high and were capped by intricately carved leaves, vines, and flowers. Each detail was painted in gold. Everywhere I looked, I saw red and gold. Seating for the congregation was much larger than the village population warranted; the long pews could fit well over five hundred worshippers at one time. I wondered from how far away people came to attend mass because there could not have been more than a couple hundred residents nearby.

This faith was something we all had in common, and though I could not discuss current affairs with my Vietnamese family, I could at least pray in Vietnamese.

When we returned to the house, our American contingent sat down to dinner with Aunt Hai, her son and two daughters, and two "uncles" from the village. I tried my best not to think of all the *Dog Meat Served Here!* signs we had passed on our ride from the airport that morning. *Dog Meat Served Here!* I must have seen that pronouncement every ten minutes. Maybe it was jet lag already seeping into my brain, but the more signs I saw, the less they shocked me. In the car, I had guessed that when they could not afford beef or pork, maybe it made sense to have dog meat.

But sitting in front of all these unidentifiable meat dishes was an entirely different story. Just imagining them to be dog meat made me vomit a little in my mouth. Many times, from primary through high school, the non-Vietnamese kids would tease my siblings and me about eating dogs. I was offended by their accusations and taunts, never wishing to believe that anyone ate dog meat. Now here I was, sitting in front of my first proper meal in Việt Nam, fearing and praying to God I wasn't dining on dog meat, and there was no way to politely inquire so as to dispel my fears. But I was hungry, damn it. I threw caution to the wind and dug in, taking mostly vegetables and only a few morsels of meat. *Tastes like chicken.*

I decided I wouldn't ask what we were eating. Though we were very likely having chicken or pork, it was better not knowing.

*   *   *

After dinner, Mom told me I could go to the back room to shower. The shower was a little room the size of a broom closet, with tiled flooring and drainage along the back wall. I hung my clean clothes on the hook on the door. After stripping, I was left standing and wondering what to do about my dirty clothes. "There's not even a second hook to hang up my dirty stuff," I muttered.

"Everything OK in there?" I heard Aunt Hai ask from the other side of the closet.

"Fine, fine!" I replied, then kept further thoughts to myself.

I ended up hanging them from the loose knob. Showering consisted of using a small plastic tub to scoop captured rainwater from a large plastic tub and pouring the water over my head. It was cold and not at all luxurious like the shower I had imagined as I soaped up and dumped more water over myself to rinse off. The cold water left my skin feeling slick instead of squeaky clean. Showering in Việt Nam sucked. I missed my tub and shower at home, with its proper curtain, clean floor, enough room to move around, and places to put stuff. I was hot, but I still missed hot water. A proper hot shower would have made me feel squeaky clean and killed off my travel germs.

At bedtime, we pushed our suitcases and bags along the walls of the loft and plopped down on foam mats, each only about an inch or two thick, over which were these very nice bamboo mats that kept us cool. Mosquito nets had been hung, and I looked up at the bare bulb dangling from the ceiling as I thought about the long day we'd had. We had made it to Việt Nam, and over the next three weeks, we would see more of the country. I fell asleep exhausted, happy to be horizontal.

*   *   *

The next morning, we woke up when the roosters started crowing at 5:00 a.m. *Dang roosters.* It was too early for waking up.

There isn't much to do when one lives out among rice fields, except plant rice and wait for it to grow. We spent the morning going around meeting the neighbors in the village. At each house, we were introduced by Aunt Hai and my cousins. The families ushered us in, and we sat on cushions on the floor when there were no sofas, which was more often than not.

"Thank you for coming to visit us," the host or hostess would start the conversation.

"Of course, thank you for having us here. We've brought a few items we thought you might need," my mom or one of my aunts would reply.

"Thank you so much for the clothes/shoes/household necessities. We really need new shirts/sneakers/random container. Your generosity is most appreciated."

Once the items were accepted and set aside, the host/hostess would take a deep, cleansing breath, as if to fortify themselves for breaking bad news to us.

"It is so hard out here," he or she would say. "You can see we live simply, that we don't have much."

We would all sit quietly and observe their poverty, the cracks in the walls, the unfinished back rooms, the openings that needed windowpanes. Then our host or hostess would launch into a story about hardships within their own home or with a family member in some other village. As I fussed with the straw in my sun hat, I pondered the drama of each story's opening or ending.

"My mother has cancer."

"My husband died suddenly last year."

"And just like that, my sister's youngest child was left blind."

Each home had its own sad tale of struggles. We sat and listened and nodded in sympathy. At the end of each visit, my mom or one of my aunts would present the family with a small gift, a few US twenties to help them out.

There seemed to be so much sadness in Việt Nam. As we made our rounds, I wondered if there were any happy stories out there, if these people ever had any reason to laugh or smile. My cousins were stoic, never smiling, their tanned faces taut, not a single laugh line around their eyes. With each additional tale of sorrow, I understood better and better why. What was the point in laughing when life gave you no reasons to? The heat and humidity were stifling, but the sadness was suffocating.

I had always wondered why my parents never really looked happy or laughed about anything. I thought it was just because being refugees and adjusting to living in the United States made things hard. But sitting in those living rooms in Đông Xuyên opened my eyes to the idea that perhaps Vietnamese people were wired to be sad. I had spent my entire life being serious, sad, responsible, and everything else heavy, but not happy or jubilant about much. And anytime I felt the least bit of joy, guilt was not far behind. I could see my own brain might be wired to be sad, just like everyone we met in Việt Nam, and it sucked. I did not want to spend my entire life being sad. What would it take to unlearn this mentality? I had to make myself happy, or I would die miserable. But this was just day two of our trip, so my plan to live a happy life had to wait a couple more weeks.

* * *

"Would you like to go into town?" Hoa asked Cecelia and me. "We'll show you the school. We have orientation this morning, and I want to call my friend."

It was early on our third morning. We had been up since before dawn, woken again by the rooster. Now we lay about in the heat, and with nothing else to do, I thought it would be a good diversion. Get out of the house, out of the village, and see what "town" meant.

Cecelia went off with our older cousin Trang on one bike as

Hoa pulled hers from the side of the house and bid me to hop on the saddle. She would peddle me into town. I looked back and forth between Hoa and the bike, skeptical that her skinny legs were strong enough to peddle for both of us.

I had already overheard some of the villagers commenting on how we Americans were so fat. I was barely 110 pounds, wearing size two clothes. It stung to be called fat, but how else could they interpret my plump and rosy cheeks? My shiny hair? My soft arms that were bigger around than the kids' spindly little chicken legs? I had yet to really consider myself or my family wealthy because, by American standards, we weren't. We were regular, working-class people. We were not struggling in the re-mote villages of Việt Nam, but we definitely weren't luxuriating in mansions Stateside (though I will admit that Aunt Kim Liên's house was spacious at just under four thousand square feet). We weren't flying around in private jets and dining on decadent cav-iar. There was nothing we could say to dispel the notions my Vietnamese relatives had in their heads about who we were. They assumed we lived carefree lives in America. But maybe it didn't matter because, compared to them, we were actually living a life of luxury.

Full of doubt, I clumsily pulled myself up on the saddle, and Hoa peddled. The road was riddled with potholes from the rains, and every dip and bump hurt. Occasionally, we would slip a bit on loose rocks and gravel, and I was sure we would end up sprawled out on the road with cuts and bruises. "Oh my God!" I would mutter under my breath with each skid.

We eventually reached the school, and though it was not yet eight in the morning, we discovered we were too late. Orientation had already taken place, and students were scattered around the schoolyard, chatting with classmates and saying their goodbyes until the start of school the following week. I wasn't sure whether we were late because my cousins hadn't planned accordingly or because Cecelia and I had slowed their ride to school. At any rate, we had suffered nearly half an hour of bumpy roads into town only to miss what we had come for.

"Well, I guess we'll go over to the post office so I can call my friend," Hoa said to us.

"What? Why do you need to go to the post office?" I asked. Cecelia looked just as confused as I was.

"We don't have a phone at home," Hoa said, kind of shrugging, as if to apologize. "We make phone calls at the post office."

Huh. That's interesting. I thought about my mobile phone, a nifty little Nokia, for which I'd bought a cherry-red cover during my first year of law school. I stopped myself from mentioning it. "OK, let's go to the post office."

We walked into the simple whitewashed but dusty post office, where three of us stood, milling about in the center, while Hoa went up to the counter at the back of the room to inquire about making a call. Along the walls were little nooks or booths with a phone, a little shelf, and a chair in each. Hoa took up the one empty booth to make her call. A minute later, she came over and ushered us out.

"No answer," Hoa told us once we were outside, squinting in the sun. She shrugged again. It must have been a tic of hers, this shrugging.

We hopped back on our bikes, and the four of us made our thirty-minute trek back to the house, stopping at a little stall along the way to pick up some fresh fruit. We had missed orientation at the school, and then the friend my cousin wanted to talk to wasn't around to receive her call. It annoyed me that she, and we, had nothing better to do than ride bikes into town for what amounted to a sack of rambutans and jackfruit. My rear end was sore from the ride, and I spent much of the morning wondering how anyone could waste so much time going to and from places for nothing.

Then, as we got closer to home, I grew annoyed at myself for thinking we had wasted our time. I spent so much of my life "with purpose" that I had never learned to relax. For a couple of years after college, I took time to hike the trails of Mount Rainier, and I'd reveled in the peace and quiet that nature had to offer, but throughout law school, I somehow forgot to relax and slow down. So what if we had missed orientation? So what if the friend wasn't around to take the call? I needed to get away from feeling like my mobile phone was the answer, my car that zipped me around Seattle was the answer. I needed to stop believing my time was more valuable than that of my Vietnamese cousins. If they wanted to spend an hour riding back and forth to town, who was I to judge? I needed to let go of being busy and feeling important. I needed to chill out.

That afternoon, our host family went out to visit with friends and left us alone in the house. Maybe they thought we wanted a break from them. Maybe they needed a break from us. My mom and her sisters were sitting and talking. Tim and Cecelia fell asleep, and I thought of following their lead. Before I drifted off, I could hear my mom and my aunts.

"It is so hot, I want to die," my mom said. "I want to die" is a common Vietnamese phrase, but translated into English, it's full of unnecessary drama. I had never examined the phrase until I was lying there eavesdropping. I might have rolled my eyes if I didn't also feel like I wanted to die from the heat and humidity. My heat rash was killing me. I should have packed antihistamines, not antidiarrheal medicine.

"I can't believe this is how they live. Look at this place. It's four walls and a roof, but there's no real kitchen or bathroom!" said Aunt Kim Liên.

"And how about the way they think? It's like they've just given up on life," my mom replied. "There's no hope in their stories. Why hasn't anything changed?" The other two murmured their agreement.

"Are we going to survive the rest of this trip?" Big Aunt asked.

The conversation went on like that for some time. I mulled over what they said and the implications of their remarks. It would appear I was not the only one suffering culture shock. My own dismay and frustrations were rooted in my perceptions of the trip from the lens of having only ever known life as an American. Here, they were lamenting how much Việt Nam remained behind in development and mindset, how they had been away for decades and yet it seemed nothing had changed for the better.

"I think we should consider cutting the trip short if it's more of this when we get to Sài Gòn in a few days," my mom suggested. I was surprised that her shock, their shock, was so great they would choose to curtail our trip. My mom and her sisters had each lost their husbands to death or divorce, and they had survived that and moved on. Yet here they were, shaken by the poverty they witnessed and dismayed by the lack of progress they found. Maybe we all wanted to escape back into our comfortable lives in America. Who could blame us?

Just Wear a Pantsuit

I sat sweating in the pews of the village church that evening through a two-hour Catholic mass. I followed along, reciting the prayers out of habit, my monotone voice blending in with those around me. I had always felt Vietnamese church services were mechanical because we all droned and said our prayers like robots. It was an aspect of church that made me dislike Vietnamese services in the States. Vietnamese services in Việt Nam were apparently no different.

I said a silent prayer for the villagers and their bleak situations. Then I sent up a word of thanks for the educational opportunities I'd had, for my hard-earned law degree, for my upcoming move to Hawaii. I prayed for patience and understanding. I apologized to God for being cranky and grumbling about the bike ride that morning. I ran my nails over my forearms, scratching at the hives that had taken over my body, yet even underneath all the itchiness, which would eventually go away, I knew I had a lot to be thankful for and that I needed to stop whining. However lost I felt in life, not sure of who I was or where I belonged, at least I was in a position to find my way instead of believing I had to accept things as they were. I had hoped for a life-changing trip, a sense of homecoming in Việt Nam, but this wasn't exactly what I was expecting. I prayed for the strength to get through the next two weeks. I wondered whether my mom and her sisters were sending up prayers similar to mine. We had Hải Phòng and Sài Gòn to look forward to.

The city of Sài Gòn lost its moniker in 1976. Though officially now Thành Phố Hồ Chí Minh (Hồ Chí Minh City), renamed in honor of the revered revolutionary Communist leader and the country's beloved "Uncle Hồ," my mother and her sisters, and even I, who had no memory of it, kept calling it Sài Gòn. Our relatives always looked at us askance, as if questioning our daring insistence on using an old name that might even risk getting us fined or jailed because it showed our defiance of and refusal to accept the current government. I wasn't sure we would actually be targeted by the authorities, but it was really a force of habit; it was Sài Gòn when we'd left, so the name stuck, suspended in time. Now we were on our way to see it and experience it anew. I would at least make an effort to call it Hồ Chí Minh City.

Aunt Kim Liên had arranged for the whole family to fly to Hồ Chí Minh City from Hải Phòng, where we spent a couple of nights, as the two-hour flight was faster (and safer) than driving for thirty-two hours. My aunts, uncles, and cousins admitted that they had never flown on a plane and fidgeted as we waited in the terminal. I watched them peering out at the parked aircraft with skepticism and fear in their eyes. When we were ushered on board, my mom gave them instructions on how to buckle their seat belts and adjust their seats.

"What if we have to use the toilet?" Uncle Trường asked in a panic before the plane pulled away from the gate.

"There's a toilet back there," Aunt Kim Liên told him after she looked to make sure. I guess for a split second, she, too, worried whether there was a toilet.

Aunt Hai, her kids, and my uncles gripped their armrests as

the plane taxied and took off. It must have seemed like a suicide mission to them, going this fast and this high. I had flown enough that I considered myself well versed, but I could still remember the first time I flew. I was seven, and for several months that year, went for an extended visit to live with my grandmother, Aunt Kim Liên, Big Aunt, and Uncle Tuyển in Kansas. It was back when smoking was still allowed on planes. In my mind, there's Aunt Kim Liên next to me, the stench of the cigarette smoke all around, and the free food on a tray delivered right to my seat. I was in heaven.

When everyone in our party was settled, Mom, seated next to me on the aisle side, leaned over and whispered, "Take a look at those flight attendants. There's no better way to oppress women than to have them dress like that. They should be going to church in those things, not working on airplanes."

"Those things" were our native country's traditional dresses for women. Called *áo dài*, they're long and flowy, constructed of a thin material, silk for fancy ones and muslin or polyester for very basic ones, split down both sides along the legs from the waist to wherever the panels ended, typically at the knees. The dress is cut with the front finished at an angle so that the front panel is snapped closed to the right side along a seam that runs from the traditionally modest Mandarin collar to the armpit. Generously cut white silk bell-bottoms are worn underneath, so long that high heels are required or the risk of tripping is great.

The female flight attendants of Vietnam Airlines wore a powder-blue dress; heavier-than-normal white pants, almost like wool office slacks; and shiny black pumps. Mom and I watched a couple of them work their way down the aisle.

"You see, their movements are restricted by that dress. Why can't they just wear a pantsuit with a sensible jacket and comfortable shoes?" Mom said to me. I wondered how they would be able to function in an emergency. The fabric of those dresses would likely catch fire and be gone in a flash. The pumps were useless. If we went down in the ocean, the flimsy dress would get soaked, turning see-through, and the trailing panels would hinder swimming. I glanced out my window to determine if we were flying over the sea.

"How would they even save us if something happened?" Mom asked me. We were apparently thinking similar thoughts. "That's how they keep women down, you know. Make them wear such impractical things."

"Wow, Mom. You suddenly dislike the *áo dài*, or what?" I asked her. Instead of answering my question, she switched subjects. "You know, if I were a young, single woman, I wouldn't marry a Vietnamese man."

What?!

"OK . . . so I'm clear on what you just said, will you please repeat it?"

"I said I wouldn't marry a Vietnamese man if I were a young, single woman today."

Who was this woman? And where was my mother? "Really?" I asked her.

"Yes, Vietnamese men are so set in their ways. And they expect you to do everything for them. Wait on them hand and foot. It's so much work. An American man would at least help out around the house and appreciate you."

"Wow, Mom," I replied, "since when do you feel this way? Does this mean you won't give me any issues when I get married? We both know my husband, whoever he is, isn't going to be Vietnamese."

She seemed to realize the weight of what she'd revealed. "Well, I'm only saying, it's better for you if you find a good man."

After all these years of impressing upon me the need to marry a Vietnamese man, to have pure Vietnamese babies, and to perpetuate our culture and heritage, my mother was sitting next to me on a Vietnam Airlines flight, somewhere between Hải Phòng and Hồ Chí Minh City, and she had just declared the most anti-Vietnamese sentiments that ever fell from her lips. Turns out, she had become more American than she had let on (or even she herself may have thought, probably)—and on top of that, she was a feminist! Pantsuits for flight attendants. And the notion that she would forgo marrying a Vietnamese man! I was shocked and amazed, and I felt a glimmer of hope that maybe she was finally coming around to my way of thinking and letting go of some of her old-school ways.

We were quiet after that, and when lunch was served, my mom and aunts showed our in-country counterparts how to lower their trays, free their utensils from their plastic case, and eat while secured to their seats.

"But we didn't buy lunch. How much is this going to cost?" Uncle Trường asked, worrying about this unexpected meal even though we rich Americans were paying for everything on the trip.

"It is part of the ticket cost. Just eat. Stop worrying," Aunt Kim Liên reassured them.

As I ate, I watched out of the corner of my eye to see how they fared across the aisle and behind us. I kept pretending I was just looking around at everyone else. They were eating the rice and meat dish but stuffed the bread rolls and the little salt and pepper packets in their pockets. I could see one of my uncles debating whether to save his pat of butter, turning it over in his hand as he looked at it intently. Perhaps he was wondering what to put the butter on, because butter sure as heck doesn't go on rice! *It'll melt in the heat,* I thought but kept quiet. I didn't want him to know I was watching, and I didn't want to embarrass him.

As I finished my meal, I wondered what they were thinking. This was likely the first plane trip they had taken in their lives and probably the only one they would ever take. Before they boarded, they had already told Mom and her sisters that they preferred to return north by train. They may have thought they were being a burden on us and our finances, or perhaps they felt entirely out of place in the airports and on the plane, afraid of crashing or getting flown somewhere else by accident. I was sad for them, that they had traveled so little and had not ventured far from Đông Xuyên. They were truly country mice visiting the big city.

Near the end of our flight, I thumbed through the in-flight magazine and found a great deal of propaganda.

"Our country. Our responsibility."

"We are stronger when we work together."

"Good health makes a good workforce."

Vietnam Airlines was government run, so it should not have surprised me to see articles and ads about loyalty and responsibility to the country. The magazine boasted about the finest aspects of Việt Nam in its photo spreads, showing off far nicer views than I had seen in the five days we had been there.

"Historical Hue. Visit the palace. Be royalty for a day."

"Enchanting Hoi An is where you should be."

We had visited Hạ Long Bay, and that had been pretty neat, but even the tour we took there smacked of patriotic propaganda. I thought about what the guide who walked us through a portion of the limestone caves at Hạ Long had said. "If you look up there at the rock formation, you will see the form of our dear Uncle Hồ, watching over us." I did not see Uncle Hồ, and neither did Tim and Cecelia. I hoped there was at least some truth to the ads and articles and that Việt Nam really was the beautiful and magnificent country they said it was.

*   *   *

"It's the same as it ever was," said Mom, peering out the window at the buildings of Hồ Chí Minh City. We were all piled into a minivan taxi on our way from the airport to our hotel. The paint was cracked and peeling on the structures whizzing by. Most signs were handwritten. Bikes and mopeds outnumbered cars on the road. The local people looked as tired and worn as the structures they passed.

"Hmmm," was all Aunt Kim Liên and Big Aunt had to say.

Later, in our hotel room and away from our Việt Nam–based family, Mom and her sisters were more candid.

"They've had twenty-six years to change. What progress has been made?" Aunt Kim Liên asked rhetorically. "The buildings are old and dilapidated. You'd think we'd see more new homes and shops, more new cars. Why aren't people dressed better? Everything is filthy."

Hồ Chí Minh City was not as progressive and modern as they had hoped or expected. Time had marched on, yet Việt Nam was still living in the past. I didn't know what to expect, having no recollection of Việt Nam, but the sights, sounds, and smells were not a surprise. I would have been more astonished to see a modern metropolis.

Despite their disappointment, our trip continued as planned. We explored the markets and tailor shops for a few days, then took day trips from Hồ Chí Minh City to the outer areas. On our drive back to Central Việt Nam, we stopped in La Vang. We were in full swing of our "Churches, Convents, and Seminaries!" tour. Vietnamese Catholics believe that the Virgin Mary appeared in the forests of La Vang in the late 1700s, when Catholics were persecuted and killed. By her appearance, she bestowed upon the people of La Vang hope that things would get better. These days, there is a shrine, and Catholics visit and pray at the site. Folks come from all over the world to pray to Đức Mẹ La Vang (Our Lady of La Vang).

When we arrived at the shrine in La Vang, Mom took me by the hand and led me over to a statue of the Virgin Mary. It was a quiet morning, and there were very few visitors. At that moment, we were the only ones in front of the figure outside. The sun was already beating down on us. I pulled the brim of my pale-pink sun hat down over my face after wiping the sweat from my hairline. I thought we would say a couple of prayers and be on our way, but Mom had other ideas.

I have had an embarrassing problem my entire life. The medical term for it is hyperhidrosis, but it is commonly known as excessive sweating. I didn't know it had a real name, a bona fide medical diagnosis, until Google came around. I read somewhere that about one in five people suffers from this condition, but I don't know where this statistic comes from or whether it's accurate. All I know is it sucks to have a sweating problem when you're already suffering from an identity crisis.

My sweating has nothing to do with how hot or nervous I am. I sweat when I'm cold. I sweat just sitting around doing nothing. I sweat when I talk on the phone. It's such a problem that if I don't hold the phone with a towel or napkins, sweat will run down the length of my arm and drip off my elbow while I'm talking. There's nothing like a sweating problem to kill my dating prospects, and the mere idea of public speaking induces nightmares.

I have hated this malfunction in my sweat glands since childhood, and as an adult, I've periodically checked for remedies and cures. There are surgeries to stop armpit and back sweating. I can even get Botox injections to alleviate sweating in those areas, but ultimately, dermatologists have repeatedly told me my sweaty hands and feet are for life, and there's nothing they can do for me. I've complained about it and have felt it kept me from doing simple things like holding or shaking hands with someone, whether I knew them or not.

So here we were, in front of Our Lady of La Vang, and Mom said to me, "Let us pray to the Virgin Mary. She will rid you of your sweating problem."

I'm not sure whether she had given it some thought before we arrived or it occurred to her in the moment, but I had zero faith that the Virgin Mary would answer my prayers. I had been sweating profusely throughout this trip—not to mention my entire life. No amount of praying would cure me now or ever.

"Come on, Hồng," Mom implored. I looked at her blankly, trying not to roll my eyes, which would annoy her. She could see I had no faith in Our Lady of La Vang.

"Ugh, Mom," I groused. "It's not gonna work. Why bother?"

She grabbed my hands and put them out, palms up. From a small basin at the base of the shrine, she took up water that had been blessed by the resident priests and proceeded to sprinkle drops of it on my hands, rubbing the water in as she prayed.

"Pray with me," she insisted in between praying and rubbing. I stood there with my hands limp in hers, refusing to play along. Our Lady looked down upon us from her perch in the shade of the trees.

A tiny part of me wanted to believe that the Virgin Mary would cure me of this problem—that if I believed, I could live the rest of my life without all this sweating. I had always loathed that part of Catholic service when we had to turn to our neighboring parishioners and wish them peace with a handshake. Thank the Lord that these days, the church encourages us to simply look at one another and nod during cold season. The flu saved me from those dreaded handshakes. I hated meeting new people and always imagined that one day, I would opt to simply walk around with a fake hand brace in my purse that I would slap on before being introduced to anyone.

"Oh, I would love to shake your hand, but as you can see, I've broken it," I would say with pretend regret.

I thought about all the times I had put paper towels in my shoes to soak up the sweat from my feet. I once tried sticking pantyliners in my shirts to catch my armpit sweat. I had learned to wear black or white tops to better hide the sweat stains—and to carry extra paper towels and tissues with me. I was the awkward Asian chick with the sweating problem.

Standing there in La Vang, in front of the statue of the Virgin

Mary, I peered up at her face from under my hat and wondered whether she would grant me that wish. I was willing to set aside "finding myself" if I could have "sweat-free living."

Please, Virgin Mary, if you can hear me, which I know you can, of course, I would appreciate some healing in this department. Thanks. Amen.

I sighed and dried my hands on my thighs before we left Our Lady's statue to find some shade. Praying was at least better than my grandmother's method when I was seven years old. She heated up a brick and crushed marigold petals on top of it, then had me press my palms into the hot clay and flower bits to burn away my sweating problem.

I was trying hard to figure myself out, who I was and what I was meant to do in life. Having my mom try faith healing to rid me of my sweating was pitiful, but despite hating the problem as much as I did, I had gotten mostly used to it. Still, it didn't hurt to offer up that prayer. I had nothing to lose.

History Lessons with a
Side of Salted Plums

My younger sister, Hạnh, graduated from pharmacy school the same month I graduated from law school. Hạnh moved to Hawaii for a pharmacist position, and because I hadn't landed a job in Seattle, I decided to join her.

Moving to Hawaii when I was twenty-eight was like moving home—but not the home I'd known growing up. It turned out Hawaii was the home I'd been longing for all my life. I went from crying over *Donald Duk* in my law school class to basking in the warmth of a community that made me feel welcome.

Aquamarine water lapped at silky golden sand as I stretched out like a cat at Kailua Beach on the weekends. My face and arms warmed in the sunlight. Tropical breezes filled my nose with the salty scent of the sea and the sweetness of plumerias. This laid-back style of living was so unlike Wichita, Oakland, and Seattle. Everywhere I went, there were Asians and Pacific Islanders; among them were descendants of plantation workers, missionaries, refugees of war, immigrants, and vacationers who, like me, had found where they belonged and decided to stay.

More importantly, within this community were individuals blazing trails and representing the state of Hawaii long before I fell in love with it. Here were the likes of Daniel Inouye, the highest-ranking Asian American politician in US history until the inauguration of Kamala Harris as vice president in 2021; Mazie Hirono, the first woman senator from Hawaii and the first Asian American woman in the US Senate; and Patsy Mink, the first woman of color elected to the US House of Representatives and the first Asian American woman to serve in Congress. They had served in government for decades, yet I knew nothing of them when I was growing up.

I knew about the bombing of Pearl Harbor and eventually learned that people of Japanese ancestry were interned during World War II, but these lessons had been delivered separately from the entire history of Hawai'i and its people. Hawai'i was an autonomous kingdom annexed by the United States in 1898 and became a state in 1959. (Note the use of the okina ['], which is an official consonant of the Hawaiian language. When the Kingdom of Hawai'i was annexed and became part of the United States, the okina was omitted in the Statehood Act, making it the State of Hawaii.) I learned that Queen Lili'uokalani was the last reigning monarch, and until her death in 1917, she fought for the restoration of the Hawaiian Kingdom. Duke Kahanamoku, a Native Hawaiian born in 1890, was a five-time Olympic medalist in swimming who popularized the ancient Hawaiian sport of surfing. Haunani-Kay Trask was a Hawaiian activist and professor at the University of Hawai'i at Mānoa. Daniel Kahikina Akaka, of Native Hawaiian ancestry, served as a US Senator from Hawaii from 1990 to 2013.

There was so much history that I was only beginning to discover. Though my sister and I walked among people who looked like us in downtown Honolulu, as I became more aware of Hawaii's past, I was humbled by this island community, yet also relieved to feel a sense of belonging. Further, I reveled in the fact that our culinary preferences were aligned. I found like-minded people who ate rice every day, snacked on sweet and savory dried fruits, and didn't think any of it was strange or unique. It just *was*.

"Oh my God, Hong, they have so many choices here. Look!" My sister pointed to the selection of dried plum snacks in the grocery store. Sweet, salty, and a bit tangy. *Li hing mui*, or crack seeds, are shriveled-up plums, dried in a combination of spices and seasonings that create a flavor that explodes on the tongue, causing immediate salivary overload.

"My mouth is watering," I said as my eyes roamed from bag to bag, examining the colors, textures, and sizes of the many offerings.

"We have *got* to try these," she said. "I wonder which ones are good."

"I guess we'll have to do our research. Life is so rough." We smiled, knowing this was a fun and worthy research project.

The snack is called *xí muội* in Vietnamese. I ate these salted plums at home without hesitation, but around my white friends when I was growing up in Florida, I did so stealthily. Each little preserved plum was about the size of a small grape and came in a dusty-gray color or was dyed red, depending on whether they were cured naturally or preserved in an unknown red powder that would stain my fingers the way cheese puffs do with their orange color. I preferred them gray so that I could eat them without leaving evidence on my fingertips. I carried them in my pockets and took small bites when I thought my friends weren't looking.

The snack originated in China, but its popularity spread across Asia. I remember as a kid going to the specialty Asian foods store, owned by one of my mom's friends and her husband. Mr. and Mrs. Đạm sold a few varieties of the preserved plums on their shelves. For about a dollar, my siblings and I shared a big bag. I never felt like there were enough to go around.

I knew Hawaii was home when I discovered a whole aisle of salted plums at Longs, the local chain drugstore. My love of Hawaii was sealed when I found entire stores at the mall selling crack seed, a term that refers to any and all types of preserved fruit, sometimes with their pits cracked to take in more of the salty, sweet, and sour flavors. Anyone could buy them and eat them. No shame. No secret hiding places. No need to pretend they didn't exist and weren't my favorite treat in the world. When I discovered *li hing mui* in abundance in Hawaii, I felt a sense of validation.

This scenario repeated itself over and over as I slowly unwrapped the beautiful gift that was my life in Hawaii: in the *phở* places that I discovered, with the sticky and chewy mochi desserts I found at convenience stores, and with the Vietnamese baguette *bánh mì* sold at sandwich shops in downtown Honolulu, stuffed with different kinds of meat and topped with fresh cilantro and pickled carrots and radish. All the delicious treats I had divorced myself from in an effort to be normal, to be American, things I had tucked away about myself, my childhood, and my ethnic heritage—they were readily available and enjoyed by the majority of the population in my new home state.

It wasn't just a sense of homecoming and feeling welcome that I experienced; it was a relief that loving those things didn't make me less American. I was thankful and giddy to finally see that I wasn't too Vietnamese or not American enough—that who I was, the foods I ate, the languages I spoke, the way I carried myself, all those things were exactly what made me fit into the American puzzle perfectly. All around me were immigrants or descendants of immigrants who called America home. I had observed the diversity over the years, but it took witnessing Asians being themselves, *being American*, for me to be able to fit myself into that larger picture. After nearly three decades, I finally understood that to be an American, I didn't need to change or deny who I was. I was exactly as I should be. Amen and hallelujah.

Is He Black?

See you at 5 for pau hana? I texted my friend Susie, who worked at an ad agency in downtown Honolulu. It had become our routine on Fridays after work to head out for a drink—*pau hana* means "finished with work" in Hawaiian but is used to mean "happy hour"—and unwind from the week's assignments. Her office building was a few blocks away from the Nature Conservancy, where I was a contracts manager and paralegal. Susie and I had both relocated to Hawaii from Seattle at around the same time. She was Korean American and had grown up in Colorado. Her brother Mike and my younger sister, Hạnh, went to pharmacy school together, which is how Susie and I met and became friends when I was in law school.

Hey, lady! Yes! See you then, she replied. Where I was serious, Susie was fun-loving and lighthearted. She brought liveliness to my new adventure in the islands. We spent time at the beaches and bars, being carefree. Despite nearing my thirtieth birthday, I was recapturing my teens and twenties, having been too busy working and studying then to let loose.

At five o'clock, I packed up my bag, turned off my computer, and headed over to the First Hawaiian Bank building, where

Susie's office was located. "Hey, Delphine!" I greeted the receptionist when I stepped off the elevator and into the front lobby. Delphine let me pass through to the bright, open room where all the cubicles were set up. Susie was chatting with her coworkers, and I joined in their conversation as I dropped my bag. We discussed how soon we would leave and where we would go. As I perched on Susie's desk, I spotted a new guy walking by.

"What's up?" he asked rhetorically, lifting his chin in acknowledgment of our little group as he casually continued past the cluster of cubicles and disappeared through a door along the far wall.

I looked at Susie. "Oh my God, who was that?"

"You mean Albert?" Susie scrunched up her nose at me.

"That's his name? He's so cute!"

Albert was a new addition to their office. His job was to manage the agency's computers and network infrastructure. With his cool demeanor and brief appearance, I was intrigued. "He's so serious, though," Susie warned. "I don't know why you'd be interested in him."

"Is he joining us for *pau hana*? Invite him," I implored.

"Geez, lady, take it easy. I think he'll be there."

He was. Albert didn't walk with us to Indigo, a hip little restaurant and bar on the edge of Chinatown, but he joined our group a short while later. Susie introduced us at the bar as we were ordering drinks. I lingered and asked him questions. I hadn't dated anyone seriously through all my time in Oakland and in law school. I was out of practice and didn't want to screw this up.

"Hey, would you like to get coffee with me sometime?" Albert asked a few weeks later, after we bumped into each other again at Friday *pau hana*.

"Are you asking me out on a date?" I wasn't trying to be coy; I needed to be sure we were on the same page.

"Yes, I am."

Albert and I went out for drinks at Kapono's on the water-front across from his office. As we listened to Hawaiian bands play, we got to know one another. Albert was not like the blond-haired, blue-eyed guys I'd pursued throughout my teens and twenties. With a Kenyan father and Ukrainian mother, Albert was brown-skinned, with brown eyes and short wavy black hair. His shoulders were broad, perfect for playing rugby. Samoans and Fijians in Hawaii often thought he was one of them.

His accent reflected the British colonialism that was part of Kenya's history, and his word choices differed from mine. The back of the car was a trunk to me and a boot to him. The contraption for pushing a baby around was a stroller to me and a pram to him. Where I sounded like a small-town American girl, Albert sounded worldly. He had been a competitive swimmer in high school and college, participating in both national and inter-national championships.

"What languages do you speak?" I asked him. "Besides English, I mean."

"I grew up speaking Russian and Swahili," he told me. "My mum spoke Russian to us, and I grew up in Nairobi, so I learned Swahili, too."

That was the sexiest thing ever. I had found myself in the company of a multiethnic, polylingual, and intriguing man from another world. In my wildest dreams, I could not have conjured up someone as complex as Albert. Why had I ever bothered with Midwest boys? They only spoke English. They never traveled anywhere. They lived in boring ol' places like Kansas. I was officially done with all-American guys.

On a follow-up date at Duke's in Waikiki, I confessed to him after a couple of strong and sweet mai tais, "I have a sweating problem!"

"OK," he said.

"I just thought you should know. In case you ever try to hold my hand." I had given it a lot of thought, and I needed him to

know about my affliction. In my mind, my sweating problem
was a potential deal-breaker. If he thought I was crazy or over
the top for such an unprompted admission, it didn't deter him. I
had my doubts about him, however, when I learned he had never
eaten *phở*.

"Hey, let's have pho for dinner," I suggested as we walked
around Honolulu's Chinatown neighborhood a couple of weeks
later.

"What's pho?" he asked.

"You don't know what pho is?" He had lived in Hawaii for
years. How could he not have had it?

"It's some sort of soup, right?"

"Yes, it's a noodle soup that's got slices of beef and is topped
with fresh herbs. It's awesome stuff." I was trying hard not to
sound incredulous the deeper we got into this exchange.

"Would you mind if we ate something else? I don't like
soups."

"You don't like soups?" I slowed my pace to look at him,
trying to gauge whether he was joking.

"Soups don't fill me up. They're a starter, not a meal. I don't
care for them." Clearly, he'd never met a bowl of *phở*.

"What else don't you like?" I asked.

"Seafood."

Seafood. Not fish. Not shrimp. Not crab.

"All seafoods?" I needed clarification.

"Yes, all seafoods."

I loved seafood. Had grown up eating everything my dad
caught and brought home for us. Sushi was an integral part of
my diet. Food wasn't the foundation of my entire existence, but
I did enjoy eating. I was an adult now, no longer at the mercy
of food stamps and their limitations on which groceries were
allowed. I no longer lived, as Mom had put it all through my
childhood, to "just eat whatever's there to get you by." It was in
my power to consume whatever pleased me.

We were partially hidden in the shadows, the sun having set. I decided to focus on the *phở* situation. I could delay our seafood discussion, but *phở* was critical.

"You'll like pho," I said confidently. "It's not just any old soup. It's comfort food and a cure-all—perfect for hangovers." I had come too far in my journey of self-awareness and acceptance to let this go. Albert had to be on board with *phở*, or we were not going to last, and I wanted us to last. I liked him. "Trust me, OK? And if you don't like it, I won't ask again."

"OK," he said with a hint of skepticism. We walked another block over and stepped into Phở 97, one of my favorite *phở* places in Chinatown. The rich aroma of the broth enveloped us in a warm, full-body hug as we chose a table along the front window. I glanced at Albert to see if the smell overwhelmed him, but he simply settled into his seat and picked up the menu. After considering our options, we agreed to get two regular bowls with slices of rare steak that cooked in the freshly ladled hot broth. I ordered in Vietnamese, showing off my language skills, scant as they were (but he didn't know that). When the soups were delivered, I showed Albert how to add fresh bean sprouts, a squeeze of lime, then hoisin and sriracha chili sauce.

"What do you think?" I asked after he'd had a couple of bites.

"It's good," he said, then dug in for more.

*   *   *

The next day, as we discussed lunch plans, Albert asked, "How about pho again?"

"Really?"

"Yes, I've been thinking about it since we ate it last night."

If I were one to fist bump or high five a win, this would have been a moment that called for it. I had a stupid smile permanently affixed to my face after that. Upstairs one morning at the Nature Conservancy, my friend and coworker Sharon took one look at me and exclaimed, "Oh my God. I know that look. Girl, you are in love." Albert and I had only been out on a handful of dates, but she was right: I was lovestruck.

Luckily, his aversion to seafood was easily cured as well. "I ate a lot of seafood growing up. It was always cooked badly," he told me. I introduced him to sushi. Problem solved. We were on track for a long and happy life together.

*   *   *

Though my mother and I spent years drifting further and further away from each other, trying to escape our scarred past, she has an uncanny ability to pick up on any new changes in my life, especially when I've started a new job or I've gone out on a date. She seems to be tuned in somehow. It's a mystery to me, and it makes it hard to hide anything from her.

"I think I'll tell my mom about you," I said to Albert one day while we were getting ready to go out. He and I had been together for several months. We both knew by then our relationship would lead to marriage.

Mom had spoken with me by phone a handful of times during those months and always asked me for news, but given our rocky past and my lingering resentment over her treatment of me when I was younger, I evaded her, chatting only about my job prospects and the weather. Now Albert and I were living together, and it was serious enough between us that I felt I should let her know.

With butterflies in my stomach and Albert on the other side of the bed, I gave her a call. I was sure she'd been expecting this and braced myself. We started the conversation with our usual stilted opening.

"Hi, Mom, it's me, Hồng."

"Hi, Hồng. You're well?"

"Yes, I'm fine."

"Well, what's new?"

For years, at this point in the call, she would ask if I had gone to church on Sunday (regardless of what day of the week it was). I had stopped going to church regularly when I was in college. Over the years, I had grown disillusioned by what I heard at mass and what I was taught, and I just didn't feel the Catholic Church's ideology aligned with my own. I am for birth control. I am for women's right to choose if they must abort a fetus. I am for women in leadership roles. I am for gay marriage. Marriage is sacred, but it's also hard as hell. Let people in the LGBTQIA+ community marry. I'm cool with all of it.

My mom, with her sixth sense, knew that I had stopped attending mass, so she took it upon herself to hold me accountable for my sins. "Did you go to church on Sunday?" was a question I dreaded for a long time. I lied to her for many years to avoid arguing with her over it, replying yes when, in fact, I hadn't stepped foot in a church for Lord knows how long. I felt it was more of a sin to go to church when all I was doing was checking out guys or thinking about what to eat, my homework, work, anything but communing with the Lord above.

Then, when I arrived in Hawaii, I decided at the age of twenty-eight that I was done cowering to her query about my faith and attendance record. Screw it if she couldn't handle that I was going to hell. "No, I didn't go to church, Mom. In fact, I haven't gone to mass regularly since I was eighteen. Quit asking."

She argued with me, just like I knew she would, but in the end, I stood my ground and told her to move on with her questions because that one did nothing for either of our souls. She could try to save me, I thought, but I didn't want her to. Having lived with her physical and verbal put-downs for so many years, I didn't feel she was the right person to ask me about my faith in God or school me on religious beliefs. She could say extra prayers for both of us if she wished.

During this particular call, though, in response to her question, "What's new?" I replied, "I'm seeing someone."

My heart full of trepidation, I waited for her response. The last time we had discussed boyfriends was when I was at KU and she'd lectured me that I needed to marry a Vietnamese man and have Vietnamese babies. As I held my breath, I could hear the wheels turning in her head through the telephone receiver. A heartbeat, then a few more heartbeats.

"Is he Black?"

My immediate reaction was disgust that she would ask such a question. Growing up among white people, we were *yellow*. Didn't she know that asking about skin color was racist? You just don't ask that. All those years she'd lectured me about not marrying a white man. What about the things she'd said on the flight to Sài Gòn when we went to Việt Nam together? Now she was asking if the man I was dating was Black? What if we didn't work out? Next round, would she ask if he's Hispanic?

"Oh my God, Mom! What does it matter if he's Black?"

"Well, is he?" *My mother is racist.*

"He's half-Black, half-white. Is that gonna be an issue for you?" I asked, then covered the phone and said to Albert, "What the hell? I told my mom about you, and she asked me if you're Black!" He had heard a few stories about her, so all he did was shake his head. He had been through this before; I wasn't his first Asian girlfriend. His girlfriend in college, whom he'd dated for seven years, was from Taiwan. I don't know why Asians hating Black people is a thing, but apparently, it is with folks like my mother. That horrible email about Asian stereotypes included it. I think it's an irrational fear of someone different. (Doesn't it say in the Bible that we all bleed the same?) In Vietnamese, white people are *người da trắng* and Black people are *người da đen*, and then when it comes to Asians, we distinguish between ethnicities instead of by skin color.

I spoke into the phone. "Is that all you want to know?"

"Is he Catholic?" *Ha!* That was more like it.

She spoke in Vietnamese, and I typically responded in English if I couldn't come up with the words in our native language. In Vietnamese, the question was actually, "Does he have religion?" It's a tricky question, coming from her. Anytime she asks that, she isn't looking for someone's religion; she's asking if that person is Catholic. It's as if in her world, there is only one religion: hers. I've been stubborn about it with my mother before: when she had asked me in junior high school, "Does your friend Thúy-Lan have religion?" I knew exactly what she meant, but I had answered, "Yes, she's Buddhist."

"Well, is he?"

"No, Mom, he isn't," I replied, then added sarcastically, "but he went to Catholic school. Does he get any points for that?" Being so many time zones away gave me the sass to be sarcastic with her, which I would not have dared to do in person.

Her two questions about Albert turned me off. She didn't want to know if he was kind to me, if he was gainfully employed, if he was from a large or small family. My mom only cared whether he was Black and whether he was Catholic. I wondered if being Catholic would have redeemed him or if she was asking out of curiosity. I didn't have any energy or patience left to subject myself to her line of questioning.

"Listen, I have to go. I need to get somewhere. I just wanted to call and say hi." There was no sense in continuing this call if she had nothing positive to say.

"OK," she said. I tapped the end call button and threw the phone down. Why couldn't I have a mother who wished me happiness? Why couldn't I have a mother who wasn't always looking for fault?

Albert and I made our way to the car and left for the movie theater. On the road, I rehashed my exchange with my mom. He understood my frustration and said, "I'm sorry, babe."

Ten minutes later, as we were pulling into a parking space, my phone rang again. Albert cut the engine as I scowled down at my phone. It was my mother. I wanted to ignore her call, but I knew she would not leave me alone until I answered.

"Hi, Mom."

"Hi, my daughter."

"What's up?"

Silence.

"Mom, you called me. Did you forget to tell me something?"

"How old is he? What does he do for a living?"

"He's a year younger than me. And he does computer work."

That seemed to appease her, especially the word *computer*.

"He works with computers?" she asked to confirm, then added without waiting for my answer, "Good. That's good. He doesn't do manual labor. He must be smart to work with computers." Never mind that three of my brothers, her sons, worked vocational jobs for aircraft companies.

"Yes, Mom, he's smart." I smirked at Albert as he listened within the quiet car.

Silence. I could hear the wheels turning in her head again. At least she had thought of more-neutral (and normal) questions to ask and had dropped the insensitive ones. Maybe in another thousand years, she would come to accept him. I would not hold my breath for that.

"OK, Mom. I'm going into a movie now. If you think of any more questions, you can call me later."

"Bye, Hồng. Be safe."

And that was how it went when I told my mother about Albert, my future husband. At least I'd gotten it over with. She couldn't be happy for me, but I'd done my duty in letting her know about him. I was glad not to hear another lecture about marrying a Vietnamese man and having Vietnamese babies. Maybe her declarations on that Vietnam Airlines flight were genuine after all.

In the years that we've been together, my poor husband has suffered my mother's disdain in the oddest of ways. "How is Robert?" she would ask when we spoke on the phone. Though I'd said his name often in conversation, she called him Robert throughout our courtship and even did so at our wedding. "Best wishes to you and Robert," she said as I smoothed the skirt on my satin ivory tea-length wedding dress in the corridor of the beachside hotel, waiting for the ceremony to begin. "I'll be sure to tell Albert you said that," I replied. I found humor in her statement, but it was dampened by the fact that my mother had brought a Catholic priest to our wedding, in case we changed our minds and wanted a real ceremony, because the Hawaiian one we planned was not right at all. "You're sure you don't want the priest to marry you?" she asked one last time before Mark, the oldest of my younger brothers, escorted her out.

I could excuse it by saying the name thing was a slipup or a language issue, but I got the sense that by calling him the wrong name, she was actually conveying her lack of willingness to accept him for no other reason than the color of his skin. At first, I would remind her his name is Albert, but eventually, it became a joke between me, Albert, and a few of our close friends. When our son was born, my mom came out to visit and inexplicably switched to calling him Alfred. "Alfred is quite good with the baby. He does a good job of changing diapers." It was yet another of her almost-a-compliment compliments.

Albert and I were confounded by the name change but laughed it off. We'd been together so many years by then that it was of no consequence to us what she called him. At least she didn't call him "the Black guy."

I've been married to Albert for over a decade now, and it's only in the past few years or so that my mom has warmed up to the idea of him being her son-in-law. She has come to terms with the fact that we're together, we love each other, and he treats me well (far better than my dad ever treated her, but the Lord would strike me down if I ever brought *that* up with her). She has finally decided to call him Albert. "Hi, Albert!" she shouts over the phone.

She has accepted him, and I appreciate that. It's validation that I've done something right in my life, finding a decent husband, even if our Hawaiian wedding wasn't the Catholic Church ceremony she dreamed of for me. Maybe he has passed some test of hers, one that took years to complete. Albert has duly demonstrated his strength and honor and has never laid a hand on me, and that's perhaps enough to prove he's a good man. Albert has finally earned his birth name in the eyes of my mother.

My friends and I still call him Robert and Alfred on occasion; those names, and the history behind them, are too ridiculous to give up.

My beachside wedding, steeped in Hawaiian tradition—not the Catholic Church wedding Mom wanted, 2007

Relationship Status: It's Complicated

Reflecting on my friendship in college with Margo, the debutante from Chicago, and the relationships I had in school, I recognized the foolishness of my efforts to erase my Asian self through dating. I wanted the upper-crust status Margo had and the ease with which I perceived she could move through society. I wanted the protection of being with someone who was a member of the majority. Mostly, I wanted someone to like me—and whom I liked in return.

My efforts to blend, to become white by associating myself with and dating white guys, were, in essence, *hiergamy*, the term sociologists use to describe a female's desire to marry above her own socioeconomic status. Though I had assumed I was simply trying to fit in with those around me, I had inadvertently stumbled into the act of attempting to class up. Further, in my quest to date guys who would help me blend in, I failed to see that I had discounted myself entirely. While trying to erase being Asian and poor, I had devalued my entire existence. If I could not accept my skin, eyes, family, and past, how could I expect my boyfriend or future husband to take me as I was?

More than twenty years later, when Albert and I left Hawaii for the Bay Area, I worked alongside Frank, an older white man. Frank had married a young Vietnamese woman named Mai after meeting her on one of his trips to Việt Nam. When I heard about Mai, I immediately doubted her affections for Frank. I was sure she only married him to get to America. He was in his fifties and she in her late twenties. What could they possibly see in each other? How could she be with him? I couldn't imagine any other reason for Mai to marry Frank besides his money and citizenship. In my haste to judge, I neglected to notice how her actions were no different from my own back in college. I had wanted to elevate myself by dating a white guy. I assumed she had wanted to elevate herself by marrying a white man. Were we not the same, she and I?

Moreover, I questioned his motives for marrying her. I wondered if he really loved her or if he wanted someone to serve his every whim, clean his house, and take care of him when he could no longer care for himself. Did he not see that she was young enough to be his daughter? Or was he fulfilling his fetish for young Asian women? It made me ill to imagine them being intimate. I hated the idea that they were married, and I probably spent more time than I should have pondering the nuances of their relationship.

Mai and Frank had a little boy a few years after they married. Frank took care of not just his wife and son but also her family back in Việt Nam. They lived in a modest single-family home in the East Bay area. He was a happy man and often spoke of his family. She slowly adjusted to living in the United States, far from her family and friends. They were married for over a decade before Frank passed away. She was distraught when he died. She no longer had her husband, and their son no longer had his father.

I realized I had judged both of them poorly when they first married, and I had done so without an ounce of self-awareness. I did not consider what either of them brought into their relationship, nor did I think about what they may have sacrificed to be together. For her part, Mai wished for a better life for herself, but being with Frank also meant that she transplanted herself into an entirely foreign world. As for Frank, he married a woman with whom he needed a translation device to communicate, and he supported her family on the other side of the world. Their choices came with benefits as well as risks.

In judging Frank and Mai's relationship, I assigned them all the stereotypical assumptions, whether true or not, that others had likely put on me and the white men I dated, Nick and Kurt. *He's got Yellow Fever, and she's a gold-digging opportunist. She wants a green card. He wants a subservient wife to wait on him hand and foot. Maybe she hates Asian men. Maybe he has an Asian fetish.*

I had adopted the same mindset as those who stood in judgment of my relationships. I never questioned my white friends' relationships. I didn't think to scrutinize Margo and her boyfriend's relationship the way I had automatically picked away at Mai and Frank's. If I, as a fellow Asian woman, could not check myself in such thoughts and opinions about mixed-race couples, how could I expect anyone else to refrain from doing the same? How would I and other women of color ever feel our relationships were authentic if we were always examining them, or being examined ourselves, in those terms? Not everything is race based, and not everyone has sinister or selfish motives for dating someone. I needed to stop subscribing to this self-defeating and harmful way of thinking.

It wasn't until I met Albert that I found someone I truly wanted to be with. Albert was completely different from the guys I had pursued in high school and college. Over the course of my twenties, I had managed to shed the idea that I needed to date the mythical all-American guy. My time away from the Midwest and among more-diverse populations allowed me to clear the lens through which I had viewed the world and my own choices. I started to wonder, *Did I truly try to date my way out of poverty? Or was I just choosing guys I found attractive based on what I felt society had told me to go for?* Either way, I was thankful my worldview had evolved, and I was glad to no longer operate under the idea that only white, blond-haired, blue-eyed guys were the standard of good looks and dating goals. There were plenty of other attractive men out there. I had found myself in the presence of one excellent example.

* * *

By the time I met Albert, I had gotten more comfortable being myself. I no longer tried to be white, and I accepted my history as it had played out. At my core, I was and would always be a Vietnamese refugee girl who grew up poor in Florida and Kansas, but my past didn't have to hem me into whatever tragic future people assumed I would have. I had the power to change the course of my life, and Albert felt the same way, not just about himself but about us as a couple.

With my husband and two boys, I don't feel the crisis of culture or ethnic identity that I felt before they came into my life. And as I've gotten older, I've learned to let go of the need to seek validation from others. I do things because I want to, not because I need anyone to compliment me. It's a good feeling. The four of us make up the diverse and dynamic family unit that I believe will allow our sons to thrive and become inclusive, confident, and empathetic global citizens.

Albert and I make a point of discussing race and culture, and we talk about politics and current events, not just between the two of us but with our sons, too. Living overseas has also given us the added advantage of being able to examine life in the

United States from the perspective of those who don't live there. We promote open-mindedness and inclusion, and we always remind ourselves to walk in other people's shoes.

"Is he Black?"

He's brown, actually, but he's so much more than the color of his skin. And I'm so much more than the color of mine.

It's Hong, Like Hong Kong

It took moving to a state where Asian Americans were the majority for me to finally feel comfortable in my own skin, surrounded by people who had almond-shaped eyes and dark straight hair, people who ate rice at every meal and enjoyed beans as a dessert instead of in chili or soup, people who rattled off their ethnic backgrounds with pride. Here was a majority population who ate pungent kimchi and meditated with gastronomic satisfaction over piping hot bowls of perfectly seasoned *phở*. They did these things not as stereotypes but, rather, in ownership of their heritage.

There were certainly still riffs between the various ethnic groups, jabs and jokes about the quirks of each—the Chinese were always pinching pennies, and the Portuguese were always talking too much—but with so many mixed-race individuals and families in the Hawaiian Islands, it was easy for me to fall in love with being nearly the same as everyone else. I was at peace, enjoying the sights and sounds of all these Asian cultures blended into one. White folks were the ones struggling with race identity in Hawaii. White people were the ones feeling the angst and confusion that came with being in the minority. It must have

been so disconcerting for white tourists who had lived their entire lives in the luxury of being the majority to be made aware of
just how many nonwhite people there were in Hawaii.

I learned a few words and phrases in Pidgin, or Hawaiian
Creole English—a mix of English and various words and phrases
from Hawaiian and the many Asian languages regularly spoken.
I knew enough to recognize what folks said, but I didn't dare
use it too often in conversation, for fear I'd be marked as a disrespectful foreigner faking it as a local, which, really, I was. Over
time, I relaxed my tongue and allowed myself to use the most
common words, *da kine* (akin to *thingamajig* or *whatchama-
callit*), *brah* (brother), and *slippahs* (slippers or flip-flops), but
I couldn't bring myself to say *mines* (the possessive *mine*, as in
"that car is mines").

Despite being a mainland Asian, I was readily accepted in
Hawaii and found myself thriving. I had never been happier, and
it showed not only in the glowing tan I got from weekends spent
at the beach but also in the way I bounced when I walked and
how I gushed about the joys of living in paradise to my college
and law school friends, all of whom were amazed by the striking
change in me. "Who are you, and what did you do with Hong?"

Nguyễn Thị Thu Hồng. For thirty years, I lived with that name.
Hồng means "pink" or "rose." It's a common and pretty
name for Vietnamese girls, but I didn't like it when I was young.
I even went through a phase when I avoided wearing anything
pink. I grew to hate my name because everyone seemed to have
trouble with it.

"What did you say your name is? Han? Holly?"

"It's Hong, like Hong Kong. And Nguyen, like 'win the
lottery.'"

"Oh, Hong, like Hong Kong. Can I call you King Hong?"

I got stupid remarks like that, and they got old.

Though I worked at the Nature Conservancy as a paralegal
and contracts manager, I pursued acting, on the side, in local

television commercials. Here, Asians weren't sidekicks or ex-
tras. Seeing myself and other Asians on television and in news-
papers further shifted the way I viewed the world and where I
fit in. In the islands, we were in every corner of the community,
from the grocery stores to the government offices. It felt good to
be more than just an afterthought. I had viewed myself that way
most of my life, and I was glad to change my way of thinking.

Still, I wanted an easier name. I was in the company of
Asians named Sharon, Melinda, Sam, Kim, Kenny, Mike, Susie,
Wayne, and Veronica. I had known most of my life that I wanted
a different name and regretted the missed opportunity to change
it when I received my certificate of naturalization. "Dear Mr.
Hong Nguyen" on a rejection letter in reply to a job application
always grated twice as much as it should.

Over the years, I had learned that a Western name offered
more access and credibility. I gave names like Holly, Diane, and
Rose at restaurants. I didn't need the host or hostess butchering
my name to a crowded waiting area. Worse than having my name
mispronounced were the assumptions made about me based on
my name. As Hồng Nguyễn, I was immediately labeled FOB
(fresh off the boat), referring to the later wave of Vietnamese and
other Southeast Asians who escaped by boat to avoid political
persecution.

In high school, I learned not to give my name when I called
businesses or government offices. It was inevitable that they
would dismiss me right away, frustrated that they couldn't understand or spell my Vietnamese name. "What did you say your
name is? Holly Winn?" I would feel insulted when, after a call,
I would meet them in person, only to have them blurt out, "I
thought you were white when we spoke on the phone!" As I got
older, I began to find humor in their shock and satisfaction in
having upended their notions of how a Vietnamese person would
sound speaking English.

After two years in Hawaii, as I was embarking on a career

in real estate, I decided it was time for a new name. I took it seriously: I browsed baby name books, I searched online for the meanings of names I liked, and I asked my coworkers and friends for their opinions.

"Sharon, do you think you could call me Diane?" She would shake her head. *Not Diane, then. Also, it would be awkward since I have a niece named Diane.*

"Michelle, I'm thinking of going with the name Michelle." She agreed that was the perfect name.

One evening, I came across an article about the importance of having a name that started with the right letter. According to a study by economists, successful people tended to have names, whether first or last, starting with *A* or *B*. Given that names were listed alphabetically, a good last name was key. I couldn't quite work on my last name, having decided that I would consider that change when Albert and I eventually got married, so I put my efforts into a solid first name. Students were nearly always called in order based on their first names, so those with *A* and *B* names were always first. *I had better get one of these* A *or* B *names.*

Having been misgendered so often as Hồng, I settled on a distinctly feminine name, one that rolled off the tongue and sounded nothing like my old name.

"How about Alison?" I asked my friends. "Yes!" they exclaimed. "What a great name!"

As Alison H. Nguyen, my business cards and website profile boasted a headshot of me, sporting my trustworthy smile. I was a real estate agent with a familiar Western first name and a common Vietnamese last name. It was a nice balance of Western and Asian. I was a safe bet for Hawaii homeowners who wanted a successful real estate transaction.

"It's such a pleasure to meet you. I'm Alison Nguyen!"

By the end of my first year as a realtor, I won an award for excellence in sales and customer service, and I believe the confidence my new name gave me helped. There was no sense of embarrassment as I said my name. Occasionally, I'd be called Ali or Alice, but I gleefully took those over the confused looks or jokes I had heard all my life. In the past, I had gotten a lot of Hong Kong, King Hong, Hong Dong, Ding Dong. Oh, the variations were endless when I was growing up. Alison didn't bring with it any teases. The worst anyone could do with Alison was sing the Elvis Costello song, which I didn't mind.

I continued to introduce myself as Alison, and a few years later, after Albert and I were married, I petitioned the court for a legal name change. I was ready to take on his last name, Lihalakha—and to permanently become Alison. As I completed the paperwork, I realized how monumental this change was and had to stop to reflect on how it would affect me.

Having the most common Vietnamese last name, I had always feared I would end up marrying someone named Smith, Jones, Brown, or Johnson, so it was in my husband's favor that his last name was none of those. I wasn't going from one common surname to another. Lihalakha, with its silent *k*, is an otherwise phonetic name that rolls off the tongue like a gentle song. Kenyan in origin, it sounds Polynesian. This was a lovely new last name for me.

Even while I gleefully dove into this name change, I still felt guilt for shifting my birth name aside and knew I needed to get over it. Historically, people have changed their names or westernized them when they emigrated to America. These name-changers knew it would benefit them, and I was simply late to the party.

I didn't want to be Vietnamese when I was Hồng, but as Alison, I find I'm not hung up on my ethnic identity like I had been in my younger days. By the time I took on a new name, I had come to accept myself on the inside. I guess it's not so much a denial of my heritage as it is a coming to terms with being Vietnamese and American simultaneously.

These days, I've taught friends how to make *phở* and shared anecdotes about growing up Vietnamese in America. I've laughed about using rice as glue for school projects. I've rolled my eyes at newfangled healing methods like coin rubbing (using a coin to scratch Tiger Balm into the skin) and cupping, all the rage now. But as a child, I lived in fear that my teacher or doctor would report us to child protective services when my back was all red from Mom's home remedies. As Hồng, I was never comfortable enough in my skin to find humor or irony in them or to accept them as part and parcel of my Vietnamese heritage the way that I do now.

It's good to shake off the stress of my childhood, to embrace the idea that I can start over, to look ahead at what can be instead of what was, to rethink what I have been through, and to release the burden of grudges and faults. Life is more fun, easier, and more adventurous as Alison. Thank goodness for new names and new beginnings.

Bank Loan for a Getaway Boat

In the summer of 2018, Albert and I were on vacation in Colorado, celebrating my cousin Bình An's start of medical school. In the shade of my sister Hạnh's back patio, we sat watching the kids play. "We" included Albert and me; Hạnh and her husband, Jason; and Albert's brother, Tony, and his wife, Carlene. Bình An was there with his parents, as were our maternal uncle Tuyển and his wife, Phương. Our children and their cousins, aged two to ten, played in the grass among the planter boxes overflowing with tomatoes and climbed the wood-framed swing set on the opposite side of the yard.

I had been writing my memoir for over a year and was talking about it with Hạnh and Albert. "You should ask your uncle how your family came to the US," Albert said. Uncle Tuyển had been with my immediate family on our journey. He is seventeen years older than me and has always been a steady and calm voice in our extended family. Ever practical, he studied to become an engineer, and he spent his entire professional career working as a structural engineer for Boeing, retiring in 2017. Now, when we see him, he's often wearing hiking gear, as if he's just coming from a hike or headed out for one, even if that's not the case.

As we enjoyed the afternoon together, he was in gray cargo pants, a plaid button-up shirt, and one of his many ball caps. His character is as relaxed as his wardrobe—comfortable, easygoing, and ready for rain or sunshine.

"You want to know how your family left Việt Nam?" he asked. "I'll tell you." His voice, like mine, is a bit nasally.

We all looked at him expectantly as he took a breath and began. "In the early 1970s, your dad had been fishing for several years, but with the political unrest in Sài Gòn spreading to the villages, your parents felt uneasy about the future.

"Your dad had joined the Popular Force, which was essentially villagers armed by the South Vietnamese military to fight the Communists. For him and others like him, their job was to protect the villages and their families." I thought my dad had fought as a member of the military. I didn't know about the Popular Force, but it made sense to have the locals do their part to protect what was theirs.

"Did you also serve in the Popular Force?"

"Yes, I did. I was a nineteen-year-old student at the time. I was handed an old World War II M2 carbine. Fifteen minutes of training and instructions, and I was a newly minted member of the force."

"Training was thorough, then," I joked. It was hard to picture my mellow uncle as a young man holding a gun.

"There was nothing to it," he said. "They showed us how to shoot at trees and sandboxes to get used to our guns, and we each got sixty bullets for our firearms." I imagined a ragtag group of villagers with guns slung over their shoulders, stashing bullets in their pockets.

"Your mom had a feeling that the situation was not going to get better. She had heard about people getting into their boats and leaving Việt Nam. It was a good way to escape communism. Your parents didn't have much money then. It was not ideal, wanting to leave but not having money to escape. Your mom cleverly decided to take a microfinance loan from a government bank. They were offering small development loans to help keep the economy going. She used that loan to build a new fishing boat. It took many months, but when it was finished, it was one of the biggest fishing boats in the village."

That *was* clever of my mom. She was twenty-six at the time, had three kids, and was pregnant with her fourth. I marveled at how, even with her limited education, she was so street savvy and willingly took this risk. When I was twenty-six, I was a single college graduate, bumbling along, trying to sort myself out.

"How long was the boat? How big was it?" I asked.

"It was long, maybe fifty feet. She wanted to fit the family and a few others. You see, she figured that if things got bad in the village, we would all get on the boat with food and water to last several days. We'd go out and stay at sea until the situation died down. There had been fighting in nearby villages, and the fighting was getting closer and more frequent. And if things got really bad, we'd go for good.

"It was a good fishing boat, outfitted with a Yamaha engine and cold-storage space. The night of April 28, we all got on board—your parents, my older sister and her husband and son, my parents, and my grandmother. There were cousins, too, and a lot of the villagers who got on the boat as well."

"Even though it wasn't their boat? They did that?" I exclaimed. I was two years old at the time, too young to remember any of this.

"Yes, it was a desperate situation. In the chaos, instead of your family and our relatives and their families, the boat ended up with about a hundred and fifty people in all. It was really too many people for the boat, but everyone was anxious to get away, and so the boat left shore just like that—weighed down by people and whatever they could take with them."

My immediate family and extended family might have totaled eighty or so, which meant nearly half the folks on board were unrelated to us. I have learned over the years that we are culturally conditioned to handle social issues either as individuals or as a collective, which influences how we respond to dealing with our needs versus the needs of our community. For Vietnamese people, the community takes precedence. It made sense that my parents would not throw strangers overboard. Americans tend to be individualistic. I could not imagine that scenario working out well if it had occurred in the United States.

"What happened then?"

"Well, it wasn't comfortable, but we stayed out there on the water overnight. In fact, it had become common practice for owners of fishing boats to take their vessels and stay several hundred feet away from the shore to avoid the theft of unattended boats.

"In the morning, my dad—your *ông ngoại*—was concerned about our house, which was in another village ten kilometers away. He said he felt it was not secure since no one was there to guard it. A few of the families on board also decided to return to shore. There weren't any onboard toilets, and they grumbled because there wasn't a plan. They left the fishing boat by dinghy, and my dad went with them. Unfortunately, ten minutes after the dinghy reached shore, a rocket was launched so close to the village that we panicked, and your father took the boat out, leaving them behind."

I imagined those who were old enough to understand were frightened and in a panic. It must have been terrifying and chaotic, watching from the boat as the rocket hit.

"Oh my God. Weren't you shocked and worried about Grandpa?" I asked, then added without waiting for his reply, "I always thought Grandpa was already sick, so he stayed behind. I didn't know he was on the boat with us." Hạnh and I looked at one another, recognizing that we knew so little of our grandfather's story. This was a revelation for us both.

My uncle replied, "We were concerned, but we couldn't go

back and risk putting everyone in danger. My dad was set to go
with us, but that's how it turned out. He wasn't sick then, but he
had a drinking problem, and his liver went bad. He died in 1977."
    My poor grandmother was on the boat with us. She must
have been devastated to lose her husband that way and without
even the opportunity to say goodbye after he returned to shore
that day.

    "What about Aunt Kim Liên? Where was she when we
left?" I knew Aunt Kim Liên had stayed back with Grandpa, but
I didn't know why she wasn't mentioned.

    "Your aunt was working as a head nurse at a hospital sixty
kilometers away. She couldn't come with us, so we ended up
leaving without her."

    I had so many questions, it was hard to choose which path to
take. I decided to follow our journey at sea. I would revisit Aunt
Kim Liên's story later. "Once Dad took the boat out to get away
from the rocket attack, what happened next?"

    "It was early morning still, around six, when we left. As the
morning progressed, the seas got choppy. A storm was brewing.
We had no plan, no idea where to go. Your parents' boat was
crowded, and as I said before, there were no facilities. It was not
ideal. We continued on.

    "Then, at three in the afternoon, we spotted a long commer-
cial ship, one of those transport-type vessels. It was called the
Trùng Dương. There were six soldiers in civilian clothes among
us, and they had a cache of weapons with them. After speaking
with your dad, one of them decided to get the ship's attention by
shooting a couple of rounds from the bazookas on board."

    "There were bazookas on board our boat?" How did Uncle
Tuyển not share that detail until now? We had soldiers among us
and weapons on board? I had imagined a huddled mass of weary
civilian villagers. Hạnh glanced at me with her eyes wide, and I
knew she was as surprised as I was at this tidbit.

    "You see, these are the juicy details folks want to know

about!" Albert exclaimed as he grabbed fresh cold beers and water from the cooler for everyone. He was only missing popcorn.

"Yeah, the soldiers had all kinds of weapons, and so they shot off the bazookas."

I couldn't believe what I was hearing. "Wasn't that dangerous? How would the commercial ship know our fishing boat wasn't trying to attack them with rocket launchers?"

The kids screamed and laughed as they chased each other in the grass, oblivious to the story unfolding at the adults' table.

"The soldiers on our boat didn't shoot directly at the ship, but away from it, and that worked because they stopped, and we were able to draw our boat close. General Bùi Thế Lân was on that ship, along with his family and about two hundred Vietnamese marines and many of their families. The owner of the *Trùng Dương* was also on board with his family.

"When we approached, the marines drew their guns. 'Toss your weapons overboard!' they shouted. They didn't want to take any chances with us, but we shouted back, telling them who we were and why we were out at sea. Once it was clear we meant no harm, they demanded again that we do as instructed. When our weapons were in the water, they lowered the net. We grabbed our belongings and scrambled for the ship."

My sisters and I had been lying all those years without knowing it. In my vague recounting of how our family got to the United States, I had always told people that we were picked up by a US naval carrier, which is what I thought had happened. It's even what my older sister, who was old enough to remember, told me when I was in college working on my thesis. How fortunate we were to have crossed paths with this transport vessel because, as it turned out, General Bùi Thế Lân was the commander of the Republic of Vietnam Marine Division fighting alongside the United States. His presence, along with that of his men, offered us security in our journey. We were now more than just refugees and half a dozen armed soldiers in a fishing boat: we were refugees flanked by members of the military. With them, we were safe from pirates and rough seas. The general must have been formidable because my uncle remembered his name without hesitation and was able to tell me he settled in Houston and died in 2014 at the age of eighty-two.

"Did anyone remain on the fishing boat? What happened to it?" I asked Uncle Tuyền.

He gave a small laugh. "We *all* got on the ship! No one wanted to be left behind. The rope that kept your parents' fishing boat tethered to the ship allowed it to be tugged along for a short while; then the *Trùng Dương*'s captain declared that the choppy waters were too much trouble, and he ordered for the rope to be cut. It was time to abandon the fishing boat."

"That must have been tough for my parents."

"Actually, your dad's brother-in-law Thái was the one who had a hard time letting go. The captain said the only way we would keep the fishing boat was if one of us held on to the rope. After the rope was cut, Thái hung on to it for a minute or two before he realized his efforts were futile. In the end, he released his grip, and we watched the boat get smaller as it drifted away."

My adult mind considered the money, materials, and plans that had been required to build that boat. I thought about the blood, sweat, and tears from the villagers that had gone into completing it. At least my parents didn't have to repay the loan on their getaway boat.

Uncle Tuyền took a sip of water from the bottle in his hand and continued his story. "We arrived in Singapore the next day," he remembered. "The Singaporean government refused to let us disembark, however, and we remained on board for a week, desperate to get off the ship. Each night," Uncle Tuyền said, "we sat on the ship and watched as people went about their business on land. Negotiations went back and forth, and the ship was refueled and supplies were replenished. We then sailed on to the Philippines."

I guess having the general on board wasn't enough to influence another country's government to accept us.

"It took a week to reach the Philippines, and there, we faced the same problem. People were getting upset and restless. We had been sailing for two weeks by this time, and folks on our ship threatened to jump overboard. We were so determined to prove how desperate we were for freedom, to get off that ship. There was a chaplain on the ship, and he declared that he wanted a plank to be set up so that each day, one of us would walk it and drop to our death in the water below to show that we were willing to die rather than stay on that ship indefinitely. My grandmother was the oldest passenger among us. She was in her late seventies then. People were saying she would be one of the people to walk the plank. It was a terrible idea."

I remember my frail and wrinkly great-grandmother. She died in Lawton, Oklahoma, in 1978, before my brother Mark was born. Her photo had hung on the walls in the houses I grew up in. We would sit together and pray for her on the anniversary of her passing, a tradition that we practiced for all dearly departed family members. It didn't seem to me that the chaplain's strategy was worth sacrificing my great-grandmother's life, or anyone else's, for.

We were in the Philippines for a week. They could not be convinced to take us despite the uproar and protests. As in Singapore, the *Trùng Dương* was forced to move on after fuel and supplies were acquired. By then, the US government had established efforts to take Vietnamese refugees, so we sailed to Guam.

"Once we got to Guam, anyone not related to us went their own way. With so many people in the camp and thousands of tents, it was impossible to keep track of anyone, much less stay in touch."

I imagined it wouldn't have been easy. This was all many years before mobile phones, the internet, and social media.

"We were just glad to be on land after a month on the *Trùng Dương*. We were relieved to have somewhere to go. When we all got on your parents' fishing boat, it wasn't as if we had any idea that that was the last time we would see our homes."

I thought about my grandfather and Aunt Kim Liên back in Việt Nam and wondered at the turmoil they must have felt once they understood we were all gone. There would have been no way to communicate with them.

By the time we reached Guam, I later learned in my research, US efforts to process and relocate Vietnamese refugees were in full swing. The military had cleared away over four hundred acres of jungle to erect more than three thousand tents, two hospitals, and nine galleys. Toilets, showers, and electricity were installed. Tent City was a major and swift undertaking that required more than twenty thousand military personnel to accomplish. We spent a month in Guam.

My uncle continued, "At the end of June 1975, the US State Department completed our paperwork, and we boarded a chartered Boeing 747."

"A plane full of Vietnamese refugees?"

"Yep, a plane full of Vietnamese people who didn't know what to expect. We landed at Fort Chaffee in Arkansas, and from there, the government found sponsors for us."

This part of the story, I knew. I had looked up Fort Chaffee on a map in college, and then when Google came around, I spent time online reading up on the place where we first landed in the United States. I didn't remember anything from that time, but when I was in high school, I found a tiny photo of my dad holding me. The photo was taken in Guam or Fort Chaffee—I'm not sure which—but it was photo documentation of our journey, snapped by a State Department employee, and one of the few pictures of my dad that stuck in my mind. I wonder what happened to it.

"Your family ended up in Broken Bow, Oklahoma. Your parents were sponsored by a chicken farm. In fact, that farm sponsored about two hundred families out of Fort Chaffee. Your mom's first job in the US was inoculating chicks. She didn't care for it at all, standing for hours and sticking needles into baby chickens. After about five or six months, your parents insisted on moving to Lawton, where I had gone. By then, I'd learned to drive a car, and with my sponsor, I drove to Broken Bow. We picked up your family and drove you back to Lawton with us."

This was all news to me. First, I thought we were sponsored by a Catholic family, not by a chicken farm. Second, I had assumed my mom was unemployed when we first came to America. My sister Hạnh was born just shy of three weeks before we left Việt Nam, which meant Mom was carrying out her fishing boat plans while she was pregnant. Then, with my baby sister, we left Việt Nam on a trip that took a month by sea. Hạnh's first few months of life couldn't have been more eventful. I felt terrible for my mom, thinking of her needling chicks all day in a foreign land while she had a baby at home with Grandma.

"The only jobs to be had in Lawton for your parents were dishwashing," Uncle Tuyển continued, finishing his story. "Your dad was a fisherman, so you all moved to Florida."

It was getting late, and we needed to clean up. I looked out over my sister's backyard and watched as the kids played. They were so young and carefree. I had a hard time processing that I wasn't even my son's age when all this happened to me. Here we were, enjoying the evening by a firepit in a suburb of Denver, so far away from that time in our lives. How fortunate we were to be employed, comfortable, and settled.

* * *

Two years later, as I was wrapping up my memoir, I talked to Uncle Tuyển to follow up on some details.

"When did you sponsor Aunt Kim Liên?" I was finally coming back to my aunt's journey.

"I didn't sponsor her, Hồng. She escaped by boat. Your aunt made six or eight attempts to escape Việt Nam after our father died. One attempt proved nearly fatal and was so traumatic, she vowed she would not try again."

I was stunned. My aunt had never shared how she came to the United States, and over the years, I assumed she easily immigrated once Uncle Tuyển was settled. It had been entirely possible for me to have never known my favorite aunt, and that idea unsettled me.

"How did you communicate with her?" I asked once I had gathered my wits again.

"We wrote letters back and forth. She used coded language in her letters to us."

"Do you still have those letters?" I longed to read them, to see the coded words, to glean from the pages whatever fear and anxiety she felt.

"I kept them in a bag, but they got lost at some point. I don't have anything from then. I don't even have a birth certificate," my uncle replied.

Too bad. Those letters were historical documents worth saving and examining. As for his birth certificate, I could relate to my uncle's remark about not having one. My parents had stashed jewelry and gold in their clothes and bags, but not our birth certificates. It's a common story among refugees. When leaving in a hurry, it's easy to forget important papers.

I asked my uncle how Aunt Kim Liên finally ended up in the States.

"Your aunt had another opportunity in 1980, and she took it, managing to escape on a small boat from Rạch Dừa, a village in Vũng Tàu. From that small boat, she and her fellow escapees were picked up by a merchant ship and taken to Singapore, where they had eventually agreed to take in refugees for processing. With our addresses in Lawton, Aunt Kim Liên petitioned the US State Department and was reunited with us a few months later."

Aunt Kim Liên's arrival in 1980 closed the circle for my family because we were all together again. In my mind, her journey was easy, uneventful, and smooth. I didn't know she nearly died trying to escape Việt Nam. She has always been focused and composed. It never occurred to me that her story so closely mirrored what the Southeast Asian students had shared with me for my senior thesis at the University of Kansas.

So that was how we journeyed to the United States from the tiny fishing village of Bến Đá, Vũng Tàu, in the final days of the conflict in Việt Nam, known as the Vietnam War to us in the States and as the American War to the people we left behind.

With Uncle Tuyển's words swirling around in my mind, I reflected on all the times I felt ashamed of my Vietnamese name, culture, holidays, and foods. I thought about all the times I could have shared my ethnic heritage with friends but chose not to. I recalled how I longed to be white for so many years, and I realized the magnitude of what I had missed out on by not knowing how my family got to where we were. I had not appreciated the folks who sponsored and welcomed us with open arms, helped us settle in and find work, enrolled us kids in school, and showed us how to shop for groceries. In my naive childhood and adolescent mind, I failed to see the efforts of all the individuals, organizations, and agencies it took to get my family and me, along with hundreds of thousands of other refugees, to the United States and other countries in the world.

I wrote this memoir because I wanted to share how much I struggled with accepting my culture and identity. In telling my story, I have learned to embrace my past and all that my parents did, all that they suffered and experienced, to get me here. I have learned to embrace who I am and what it means to be

Vietnamese *and* Asian American. I will certainly be more circumspect if I decide to joke around about anyone being "fresh off the boat." I believe our strength and resilience come not only from what we are doing today but what we, and those who walk alongside us, did all the days prior to get us to this point in our journeys. May all immigrants and refugees hold strong to who they are and where they've come from.

Me in my element, the outdoors, on a sunny day, 1982

Acknowledgments

I am thankful to the following people for their assistance, encouragement, and inspiration: Shari Caudron, for coaching me through many months of writing and self-examination; Diana Rico, for editing my manuscript and offering invaluable feedback; and Phúc Trần, for answering questions and offering advice about writing while Vietnamese. Thanks to the team at Girl Friday Productions for getting my story out into the world. I am incredibly fortunate to have met Norman Yetman. Thank you for being a role model and parental figure (at the University of Kansas and long after I graduated) and for starting me on my path of cultural awareness. Decades late in coming, I would like to thank my fellow university students from Southeast Asia who recounted their stories of immigrating to America and the adjustments that ensued. In a way, this is the senior thesis I promised to write and share.

Thanks to Cindy Janus, Karien Wilson, and my sister Hạnh for reading the early drafts of my memoir. Thanks to my uncle Phạm Quang Tuyển for all the details about our journey from Việt Nam—and for putting up with the clueless college-graduate version of me when I showed up at his doorstep in Seattle. Thank you to my mother for her strength, resilience, and ingenuity in tackling life's uncertainties, of which there have been plenty. Last but not least, I wish to thank my husband, Albert, and our two sons for their love, support, and cheerleading.

About the Author

Alison Hồng Nguyễn Lihalakha grew up in Florida and Kansas before heading to the West Coast and settling in Hawaii. She was the first in her family to complete a university education, graduating from the University of Kansas with honors in Sociology.

She served two years as a Teach For America corps member teacher in Oakland, then went on to earn a law degree from the University of Washington. Alison's career has included legal advocacy, contract management, and real estate sales. Her interests in children's rights and the plight of displaced persons led her to further her studies, and she earned a Certificate in International Development from the University of British Columbia.

Alison has spent the past ten years living abroad with her husband and children. In Tunisia, Saudi Arabia, and most recently the Republic of Korea, she has made friends and explored new customs and cultures while sharing her own. *Salted Plums* is her first publication.